THE
HONORED
GIFT

MARLENE BULLOCK

WESTBOW
PRESS
A DIVISION OF THOMAS NELSON
& ZONDERVAN

WestBow Press books may be ordered through booksellers or by contacting:

WestBow Press
A Division of Thomas Nelson & Zondervan
1663 Liberty Drive
Bloomington, IN 47403
www.westbowpress.com
1 (866) 928-1240

Because of the dynamic nature of the Internet, any web addresses or links contained in this book may have changed since publication and may no longer be valid. The views expressed in this work are solely those of the author and do not necessarily reflect the views of the publisher, and the publisher hereby disclaims any responsibility for them.

Any people depicted in stock imagery provided by Getty Images are models, and such images are being used for illustrative purposes only. Certain stock imagery © Getty Images.

Scripture quotations marked KJV are taken from the King James Version.

ISBN: 978-1-9736-7520-4 (sc)
ISBN: 978-1-9736-7522-8 (hc)
ISBN: 978-1-9736-7521-1 (e)

Library of Congress Control Number: 2019914310

Print information available on the last page.

WestBow Press rev. date: 10/18/2019

A bold Writers computer says, "Time to write the story!"

1

Introduction
Marlene Bullock

When I began writing, I had many challenges to face. A great mental or physical effort tests my personal success. My giftedness abilities such as faith created an atmosphere to endeavor beyond the norm. I try hard to attempt, undertake, and aim higher than my own efforts writing.

To do so, I had to take to attitude and character of writing. Habit forming arranges itself "The Untold Story" unfolded. Faith substance created a positive surrounding clarity of mind to produce the effectiveness needed to attain. The Word says, "Now faith is the substance of things hope for, the evidence of things not seen" (Hebrews 11:1KJV). "And, without faith it is impossible to please him: for he that cometh to God must believe that he is, and that he is a rewarded of them that diligently seek him" (Hebrews 11:6KJV). To determine what level of success of outcome will produce the blessing to the End. The Word says, "The four and twenty elders fall down before him that sat on the throne, and worship him that liveth for ever, and ever cast their crowns before the throne. Thou art worthy, O Lord, to receive glory and honour and power: for thou hast created all things, and for thy pleasure they are created" (Revelation 4:10-11KJV). Destiny creates power to attempt the pressure to walk by faith to produce fruitfulness. Faith is hidden effort to achieve One's completeness to wholeness in singleness of life. The task of One's journey is to endeavor until the End, because the attempts to climb mountains are snares, and pitfalls to turnabout. Writing is challenging strength with One's soul to gain knowledge to exist out of challenges to strengthen our weakness. I am learning to use aim as a weapon to train abilities of sight to aspire inspiration through opening signature writing within. Shortcomings are evitable material not necessary. And, design to escape curves of One's own viewpoint can become rewarding. A viewpoint can develop consideration importance differently between each reader. The Words says, "Go to the ant, thou sluggard; consider her ways, and be wise" (Proverbs 6:6KJV) A sluggard can be a lazy person in viewpoint, or no guide in direction. An ant is wise enough to prepare for predictable situations. In writings signature of heart One's own soul draw out of heart direction needed to fulfill the destiny dream written: Written memories fulfills void desires aching pain of long- sufferings of other need to feel love.

2

American Tradition Family

I was born to proud parents on day, June 4, 1958. Nash Harris Bullock age 33, and Frances Merle Young age 28, were Register of Deeds, Cumberland County, Fayetteville, North Carolina. Institution of Birth location was Cape Fear Valley Hospital. Fayetteville, North Carolina was a country pleasant location to live. It Settle in Year 1783, and being home of Fort Bragg, home of the 82nd Airborne and the U.S. Army Special Operations Command. My father served in the United States Military Navy Command for completion upon almost full twenty-years. He served as a Navy Command Sailor, Cook out on Sea. And, a Tile Setter trade labored. Business Owner he established in Melbourne, Florida until passing death. My mother was a housewife and seven siblings she nurtured. She provoked her children not to be angry, love and respect others. She taught us to play close nearby home. My Mother had a beautiful appearance deep inside of her that smiled with beauty. Her passing was experienced early age ten for me. And, kinship cared for me afterwards. Memory of Parent will always be heartfelt love for a daughter, and God's Creation Imaged to always live in a manner of modesty. The Words says, "I am the rose of Sharon, and the lily of the valleys. As the lily among thorns, so is my love among my daughters" (Song of Solomon 2:1-2KJV). The love for an earthly father is different than love between a daughter and heavenly Father God. The love experienced with God is a committed intimacy of wholeness mutuality. The goal is to succeed pressing into eternal successfulness completion of LIFE. God has a deep love for his people. Christ love for the Church grooms the Soul connection that separates love from the world ecstasy and fulfillment. The Book of Songs expresses the Love of God for his daughters, and the love between man and woman. And, the desired love an earthly father has for his daughter too. Inwardly, we must look beyond darken glass of our Soul to perfectly match to Love of God. The Word says, "Charity never faileth: but whether there be prophecies, they shall fail, whether there be tongues, they shall cease; whether there knowledge, it shall vanish away. For we know in part, and we prophesy in part.* But when that which is perfect is come, then that which in part shall be done away. When I was a child, I understood as a child, I thought as a child: but when I became a man, I put away childish things.* For now we see through a glass, darkly; but then face to face: now I know in part ; but then shall I know even as also I am known. And now abideth faith, hope, charity, these three; but the greatest of these is charity" (1 Corinthians 13:8-13KJV). A Covenant Agreement must be consistent with Father God, and his daughter to understand revelation knowledge. A barrier between an earthly Father, and his daughter defiles through rudiments of the world hidden underneath the surface that can create lack of knowledge of knowing revelation. The Word says, "Beware lest any man spoil you through philosophy and vain deceit, after the rudiments of the world, and not after Christ"* (Colossians 2:8KJV).Expression of Family Covenant from a daughter birthing additional siblings pictures a huge house up on a hill, and much gardening to planting much seeds of love. However, although, each role plays its own part of priorities it has an order. The total order of family form in Scripture says, "And thou shalt love the Lord thy God with all thine heart, and with all thine soul, and with all thy might" (Deuteronomy 6:5KJV). Family must put God first on regular fellowship Time shared in their lives. Secondly, if married, the spouse love comes next to closeness to be proven of the Lord. Thirdly, married couple should attend a fellowship support local body of members of Christ. The Words says, "Not forsaking the assembling of ourselves together, as the manner of some is; but exhorting one another: and so much the more, as ye see the day approaching" (Hebrews 10:25KJV). The assembling together unites the bond structure to strengthen families, and outwardly expresses adoration for God. It consists of admonition to ensure the perseverance to the endurance. The daughter's knowledge of earthly Father viewed tablets of Scripture upon my heart merely for spiritual guidance to survival. Its development recompense rewards through expression to Write of History. The Word says, "Husbands, love your wives, even as Christ also loved the church, and gave himself for it:* v26 That he might sanctify and cleanse it with the washing of water by the word,* v27 That he might present it to himself a glorious church, not having spot, or wrinkle, or any such thing; but that it should be holy and without blemish.* v28 So ought men to love their wives as their own bodies. He that loveth his wife loveth himself" (Ephesians 5:25-28KJV). Husband serve God first, then wife additional children. The woman priorities is Father God first, then her husband. Joined together by God's abilities, the family produces the measurement outcome to source of resources for a Career of Success. Parents are to raise godly children those who love the Lord with all their hearts. Of course, after children becomes adulthood, to care for own obligations. The Words say, "But if any provide not for his own, and specially for those of his own house, he hath denied the faith, and is worse than an infidel" (1Timothy 5:8KJV). Lack of knowledge it disavows a family units to neglect its own provision labor of wage to rest. The Words says, "For even when we were with you, this we commanded you, that if any would not work, neither should he eat" (2 Thessalonians 3:10KJV). God is straightforward on family conformity. My earthly Father informative instructions growing to adulthood were strictly stern to correction to benefit my success. And, past relationship with earthly Father, and present relationship with heavenly Father is continuation encouragement to my life inside, and outside family to empower all to greatness.

3

The Journey Begins

Having experience speech impediment from birth to age of five years old, developed much fear in me. These few years, I experience torment of fear seem imaginary supernatural way that only viewed Visions demonic realm activity and Angelic visitations realm of faith trusting God. The spiritual fear encounters paralyzed my language speech to talk. Special Education developed my communication skills slowly to learn. Often, I sleep in fear of the unknown about to happen, but faith level grew stronger within me to trust God more through prayer. The Word says, "The eyes of your understanding being enlightened; that ye may know what is the hope of his calling, and what the riches of the glory of his inheritance in the saints, * v19 And what is the exceeding greatness of his power to us-ward who believe, according to the working of his mighty power" (Ephesians 1:18-19KJV). I grew into a desire to fully understand the mysteries of God to a heaven destiny. The illumination was valuable information for obtaining inheritance from an unseen realm of Power existence upon Earth. At the age of six, I encountered an angelic beautiful visitation bedside divine appointment. My lips were embraced by the touch of an angel to begin my healing. The communication speech impairment lifted from my lips to shape talk words inspired me. And, I shared visitations with my siblings without doubting the appearance. The Word says, "And from the days of John the Baptist until now the kingdom of heaven suffereth violence, and the violent take it by force" (Matthew 11:12KJV). Often, I felt as a student discipline to Spirit of Truth, and much guided through leading of the Holy Spirit. The Words says, " Howbeit when he, the Spirit of truth, is come, he will guide you into all truth: for he shall not speak of himself ; but whatsoever he shall hear, that shall he speak; and he will show you things to come" (John 16:13KJV). I always felt parted to God knowing my leading was from him. Along, I continued to listen attentively. The Words says, "For to be carnally minded is death; but to be spiritually minded is life and peace. v7 Because the carnal mind is enmity against God: for it is not subject to the law of God, neither indeed can be" (Romans 8:6-7KJV). And, I constantly followed brightness appearance of visions afterwards. The Word says, "Jesus saith unto him, I am the way, the truth, and the life: no man cometh unto the Father, but by me" (John 14:6KJV). So, I inwardly kept peacefulness, but off course discouragement setbacks oppressed me. The encircled motion of faith of God of Creation Existence were spoken Words were abiding in activation upon my life. I had a "Witness" dwelling inside to walk by faith, and not by sight. The Word says, "Before I formed you in the belly I knew thee, and before thou camest forth out of the womb I sanctified thee, and I ordained thee a prophet unto the nations" (Jeremiah 1:5KJV). The Word additional says, "For he gives his angels charged over thee, to keep thee in all thy ways" (Psalm 91:11KJV). An enthusiasm vigor passion for God started flowing more into my direction for supernatural divine healing. The gift of healing for the sick moved me with compassion. The Healing Ministry of Jesus became attracted more to me. His teachings were astonishing with an extreme surprise as resolved issues would disappear before my eyes. The Word says, " For all that is in the world, the lust of the flesh, and the lust of the eyes, and the pride of life, is not of the Father, but is of the world" (1John 2:16KJV). Distractions seem to pull our attention away from the Master. When the gifts of healing are functioning correctly the emphasis results to process our faith to believing becomes Truth. The gift is not designed to produce divine "healers," but divine healing is communication to receive revelation from God. Further into revelation, I walked into realms of glory that produced more from God through prayer of faith increased. My inclination led me through a certain narrow way. The Word says, " There is no temptation taken you such as is common to man: but God is faithful, who will not suffer you to be tempted above ye are able; but will with the temptation also make a way to escape, that ye may be able to bear it" (1 Corinthians 10:13KJV). Times, I felt as if I was landing a place for a ship without water. But God always landed me onto the other side. He always kept me intact to the importance eagerness of enthusiasm wholeheartedness to cleave to him. The Word says, "Enter ye in at the strait gate: for wide is the gate, and broad is the way, that leadeth to destruction, and many there be which go in thereat; v14 Because strait is the gate, and narrow is the way, which leadeth unto life, and few there be that find it" (Matthew 7:7-8KJV). The narrow gate has a brightness of illumination! And, I experienced sudden darkness along the way. It was a distorted darkness to confused the existence to power I needed supply to embrace my fears. God always enable me with patience to obviously from being led not by wrong spirit. I figured in the darkness, God had firm grip on me and he would not drop me. In the valley of despair more passionate and more responsible to trust God through patience was the key that unlocked the next door. I realized the deep, deep ties between me and God. And, it brought much healings on my knees to our Lord Jesus Christ as the heavens open up. His richness of glory became the lifter of my head, and gave me much strength in my inner man, and soared me higher ground. The inclination learning to feel a particular way changed my natural man walking with God. As a young girl, limitations were not a problem to my development. I heartfelt my need for the love of God, and my expectations grew stronger as I trusted him. I trusted him to open my full understanding to acknowledgment of my destiny throughout the years of my youth. Previously, the urge persisted to longer length of time to praying unto God continued in my life. I searched His ways, and thoughts to my own abilities were proven change. The journey continued as the flowers grew in the garden, and the fields turned cotton white. The darkness brought fear, but the day sunlight burned bright. The Word says, "For we are His workmanship, created in Christ Jesus for good works, which God prepared beforehand that we should walk in them" (Ephesians 2:10KJV). My faith increased as I grew up! I carried my Cross and never question God.

4

Upon Arrival

At the age of eight years old, I started experiencing faith that brought an enjoyable pleasure. Often, I spent much time talking to God and sharing my joyfulness! I learned quickly to follow the instructions from Father God. The impressions of visions appearance brought me into a deeper realm through prayer. And, I recognized faith with prayer created activation strength to unknown POWER. The Word says, "Even so faith, if it hath not works is dead" (James 2:17KJV). So, I started moving forward in faith believing. The Word says, "That if thou shall confess with thy mouth the Lord Jesus, and shalt believe in thine heart that God hath raised him from the dead, thou shalt be saved. For the heart of man believeth unto righteousness, and with the mouth confession is made" (Romans 10:9-10KJV). Whenever, I practiced faith in God, and matched my faith with prayer without doubting everything changes. The Word says, "For whosoever shall call upon the Lord shall be saved" (Romans 10:13KJV). I never have had a problem learning from God, but walking by sight weaken my response to move swiftly to his voice speaking to me. It seems though sight linked chains that ring pieces to create volume of doubt in my thinking. Cautiously, I stayed the course of faith, and fought the stronghold hindering my mind to think separate from my five senses of knowing, tasting, feeling, touching, and hearing. The Word says, "For my thoughts are not your thoughts, neither are your ways my ways, saith the Lord.* v9For as the heavens are higher than the earth, so are my ways higher than your ways, and my thoughts than your thoughts" (Isaiah 55:8-9KJV). Detecting realm of the Holy Spirit helped discovered the identity of existence of the heavenly surroundings to me. I searched out the inspiration with amazement each take it appeared unto me. The Word says,

"Now the serpent was more subtile than any beast of the field which the Lord God had made. And he said unto the woman, Yea, hath God said, Ye shall not eat of every tree of the garden?* v2 And the woman said woman said unto the serpent, We may eat of the tree which is in the trees of the garden:* v3 But of the fruit of the tree which is in the midst of the garden, God hath said, Ye shall not eat of it, neither shall ye touch it, lest ye die.* v4 And the serpent said unto the woman, Ye shall not surely die.*v5For God doth know that in the day ye eat thereof, then your eyes shall be opened, and ye shall be as gods, knowing good and evil.* v6And when the woman saw that the tree was good for food, and it was pleasant to the eyes, and a tree to be desired to make one wise, she took of the fruit thereof, and did eat, and gave also unto her husband with her, and he did eat.* v7And the eyes of them both were opened, and they know that they were naked; and they sewed fig leaves together, and made themselves aprons,*v8 And they heard the voice of the Lord God walking in the cool of the day: and Adam and his wife hid themselves from the presence of the Lord God amongst the trees of the garden" (Genesis 3:1-8KJV). Early age, I felt such a pattern to continue to listen to a small "Still Voice" to follow. My ability to use my innocent hands gifted evidence that supported my leading. Often, I wander to a certain garden area cleave to God without possibly tempted to focus on wrongful acts. I was learning intelligence applied about mankind with much physical illness and sorrow of pain. Man failed under the covenant, degenerated diseases were the curse headed to him for disobedience in the Garden of Eden. The positive results from my obedience to watch as well as prayed revealed the acknowledgement continually coursed by Father God. Furthermore, I advanced into more direct information spoken by a small "Still Voice." My heart grew into desire "birth pains and sounds." I was willing to submit to him, because of the privileges and responsibilities kept evilness from penetrating my faith. Sounds of aggravation, fear, and doubt sharing of divine power formed a second woman in me. It formed me in His image, and clothed me in His righteousness. My natural stature height increased, and my love grew strong throughout the darkness to teach all mankind about faith that heals given to me. I gained encircled realms dimensional atmosphere of faith increase to make whole. It was obvious through my countenance showed inspirational sacrifice brought much joy. The inspiration grew a longing desire to reach out to mankind and fellowman. God gave me opportunity to do well, and I mannered my hands to plow for him. All my interpretation of visions appearance variation gave certain limits as trust developed. The boundaries from his hands were woven into my hands to a certain trust level that higher degree of counseling formed a crystal. It formed "blood guiltless" seriousness unto mankind to a call of repentance. I knew I had a divine connection to the act upon grace of God for tender mercies. And, the sounds of darkness to nakedness living without hope had to change. I tempted to cover nakedness of sins sharing of the divine power. The revealed knowledge of God proved that heart of man can contrast between two men. A Bible story, Nicodemus was a Pharisee, a ruler of the Jews, and a Master of Israel. Nicodemus accepted Jesus as a teacher, and a Rabbi from God. The Word says, "There was a man of the Pharisees, named Nicodemus, a ruler of the Jews:*v2The same came to Jesus by night, and said unto him, Rabbi, we know that thou art a teacher come from God be with him.*v3 Jesus answered and said unto him, Verily, verily, I say unto thee, Except a man be born again, he cannot see the kingdom of God" (John 3:1-3KJV). It takes revelation knowledge from the Commandments of God to understand Eternal Life.

5

Faith

The Word says, "Out of the mouth proceedeth blessings and curses. My brethren, these things ought not to be" (James 3:10KJV). Faith created miracles untold at early age for me. The Word says, "And Jesus answering saith unto them, Have faith in God.*v23 For whosoever shall say unto this mountain, Be thou removed, and be thou cast in the sea; and shall not doubt in his heart, but shall believe that those things which he saith shall come to pass; he shall have whatsoever he saith" (Mark 11:22-23KJV). Building stones of faith never fades away, but allow you to walk closer to God. These stones are pebbles full surfaced from growing learning to walk through loving arms to Father God. When you embrace the unseen to guide you, only the purposed destiny you have is endeavoring the surroundings to changes to a brightness of Light. I tried hard to continue to walk through the unseen achievement. The Word says, "For I know the thoughts that I think of you, saith the Lord, thoughts of peace, and not of evil, to give you an expected end" (Jeremiah 29:11KJV). The obligation constantly to making an effort is not walking away from the commitment. A determination sets boundaries to undertaking the task to our next level. Balance is required through earnestness and fair amount from effort applied. The broken building stone walked keeps our mind focus to compass direction needed. The Word says, "Wherefore also it is contained in the scripture, Behold, I lay in Zion a CHIEF CORNER STONE, ELECT, PRECIOUS: AND HE THAT BELIEVETH ON HIM NOT BE CONFOUNDED.v7Unto you therefore which believe he is precious: but unto them which be disobedient, THE STONE WHICH THE BUILDERS DISALLOWED, THE SAME IS MADE THE HEAD OF THE CORNER" (1 Peter 2 6-7KJV). The problem with faith is that it is unseen completeness of our salvation unto the End, but we are to continue our journey. Sometimes, having our understanding darkened by principalities, or worry offsets our mind. And, the focus that is needed for perspective change only develops through the Word of God. Often, perspective change encircles the compass of our direction to delay. Our mindset leaves focus to enter a warring of warfare in the heavens to doubt. The Word says, "And Jesus went out, and his disciples, into the towns of Caesarea Philippi: and by the way he asked his disciples, saying unto them, Whom do men say that I am?* v28 And they answered, John the Baptist: but some say, Elijah: and others, One of the prophets.v29 And he saith unto them, But whom say ye that I am? And Peter answereth and saith unto him, Thou art the Christ.* v30And he charged them that they should tell no man of him" (Mark 8:27-30). When an individual overcomes the stepping stones of faith he, or she will be awarded in heaven. The Word says, " He that hath an ear, let him hear what the Spirit saith unto the churches; To him that over-cometh will I give to eat of the hidden manna, and will give him a "white stone," and in the same stone a new name stone written, which no man knoweth saving he that receiveth it" (Revelations 2:17KJV). That manna represents a new life! The "white stone" symbolizes acceptance and approval of God. That completes the fullness of expectancy of joy in the Beloved. A 'white stone" with believer's name on it could also be possibly a reference to our standing in God. The "white stone" is our entrance to Victory Won is Christ Jesus! Faith eternal victory refers to the earnest working through Holy Spirit redeemed Plan of Salvation has Sealed the Promise of God. Hallelujah!

6

Confidence of Trust

earning to discern to differentiate different realms of the Spirit challenged limit tolerance to much aggravation from uncertainty. Unlimited surpassed the challenged spiritual attacks that were sent by adversary to onslaught every opportunity to my advancement. Struggling tolerated the grip to trust God to build confidence of assurance for my endurance to strengthen higher climb of height. The Word says, "That he would grant you, according to the riches of his glory, to be strengthen with might by his Spirit in the inner man,* v17 That Christ may dwell in your hearts by faith; that ye, being rooted and grounded in love, * v18 May be able to comprehend with all saints what is the breadth, and length, and depth, and height; v19 And to know the love of Christ, which passeth knowledge that ye might be filled with all the fullness of God. v20 Now unto him that is able to do exceeding abundantly above all that we ask or think, according to the power that worketh in us, v21 Unto him be glory in the church by Christ Jesus throughout all ages, world without end" Amen. (Ephesians 3:16-21KJV). The confidence needed to full circle trust takes an open heart unto heavenly Father. He sees our fallen dreams desires to search the way, but the way is narrow. The Word says, "The Lord is my light and my salvation; whom shall I fear? The Lord is the strength of my life; of whom shall I be afraid. v2 When the wicked, even mine enemies and my foes, came upon me to eat up my flesh, they stumbled and fell. v3 Though a host should encamp against me, my heart shall not fear: though war should rise against me, in this will I be confident. V4 One thing I will desire of the Lord, that I will seek after; that I may dwell in the house of the Lord all the days of my life, to behold the beauty of the Lord, and to enquire in his temple. v5 For in the time of trouble he shall hide me in his pavilion: in the secret of his tabernacle shall he hide me; he shall set me up upon a rock. v6 And now shall mine head be lifted up above my enemies round about me: therefore sacrifices of joy; I will sing praises unto the Lord" (Psalm 27:1-6KJV). David was falsely accused in deep distress. David's motives were not for revenge, but an opportunity to give praises unto God. Rather, it also was a plea for God's righteous judgment upon Saul's attack against David. That proper attitude needed for one to wait upon the Lord God to act his strength is grateful love. However, I can wait upon the Lord God, but I must give him deeper heart. The sacrifice I pay is picking up one's own Cross to follow him through obedience. The obedience is moving forward inside hidden dream of my own unknown increase needed of faith to produce it. You are not alone! Stay faithful! Rich or poor does not matter maintain to remain in the trust of love for Father God. Trust fully in Jesus name, and hope will increase. The Word says, "My little children, these things write I unto you, that ye sin not. And if any man sin, we have an advocate with the Father, Jesus Christ the righteous" (1 John 2:1KJV). An Advocate is someone who intercedes for another. God is always fighting for his children. He is a Mighty Fortress, strong in battle. The Word says, "Plead my cause, O Lord, with them that strive with me: fight against them that fight against me. v2Take hold of shield and buckler and stand up for mine help. v3 Draw out also the spear, and stop the way against them that persecute me: say unto my soul, I am thy salvation.v4 Let them be confounded and put to shame that seek after my soul: let them be turned back and brought to confusion that devise my hurt.v5 Let them be as chaff before the wind: and let the angel of the Lord chase them. V6Let their way be dark and slippery; and let the angel of the Lord persecute them. v7 For without cause have they hid for me their net in a pit, which without cause they have digged for my soul. v8Let destruction come upon him unawares: and let his net that he hath catch himself: into that very destruction let him fall. v9And my soul shall be joyful in the Lord: it shall rejoice in his salvation" (Psalm 35:1-9 KJV). An individual does not back from God without humility fear of the Lord in their heart. He will always fight for you. Because God does not back down from any standard of man. The Word says, " Not every one that sayeth unto me, Lord, Lord, shall enter into the kingdom of heaven; but he that doeth the will of my Father which is in heaven. *22 Many will say unto me in that day, Lord, Lord, have we not prophesied in thy name? and in thy name have cast out devils? and thy name done many wonderful works?* v23 And then will I profess unto them, I never knew you: depart from me, ye that works iniquity" (Matthew 7:21-23KJV). Rather, God pleads our case to defend his children's innocence. Our expression of love for him reveals the trust assurance level of love hidden for the Creator imaged designed in us. The Words says, "The righteous cry, and the Lord heareth, and delivereth them out of all their troubles. v18 The Lord is nigh thee unto them that are of a broken heart; and saveth such as be a contrite spirit. v19 Many are the afflictions of the righteous: but the Lord delivereth him out of them all. V20He keepeth all his bones: not one of them is broken" (Psalm 34:17-20KJV). Throughout the reading of the Holy Bible shows many had experience death situations, but God's arrival spared their lives through a bonded TRUST. Having confidence trust in God will endure hardships, trails, temptations, and faithful martyr. A Christian should keep their confidence trust in God alone through every satanic influence. Do not be moved! Stand in the Holy Place, and "witness" your victory! The Word says, "And I say also unto thee, That art Peter, and upon this rock I will build my church; and the gates of hell shall not prevail against it" (Matthew 16:18KJV). If the Christian realized the foundation of the church overcame "sting of death."

His church would aggressively stand up against the onslaught attacks from Satan. The glorious kingdom of God is Light, and the alignment is not offensive, but POWER OF GOD. The Word says, "And from the days of John the Baptist until now the kingdom of heaven suffereth violence, and the violent take it by force" (Matthew 11:12KJV). The indication culminating point is compass your confidence trust level higher in Father God, and watch His POWER turn it all around for your good. Additional says, "And we know that all things work together for good to them that love God, to them who are called according to his purpose" (Romans 8:28KJV). So, purpose is divine with destiny to one's successfulness. We should learn to appreciate the rewards returned from our confidence trust in God to work furthermore, because God advances greater "Eternal Weight of Glory" beyond the grave. The Word says, "Every good gift and every perfect gift is from above, and cometh down from the Father of lights, with whom is no variableness of turning" (James 1:17KJV). God is the Creator, and he is more than stable way of man. He is immutable. There is not the slightest change in God. God is always good! God says, "I hear you say Lord, here is my heart." He replied, "I have seen the fallen dreams not to search after me with your whole heart. And, I will bring you again to that place of faith that I can be glorified. Have Faith! Trust me, that I can be glorified. Trust My child, I can be glorified in Truth!" Oh God! Sweet surrender!

7

Strength

Now, the unseen privilege available strength can additionally be added through the knowledge of putting off the old man with his deeds, and putting on the new man knowledge imaged after God. We are to be constantly changed throughout fellowship with Father God. The Word says, "And that ye put on the new man, which after God is created in righteousness and true holiness" (Ephesians 4:24KJV). The Word says, "For which cause we faint not: but though our outward man perish, yet the inward man is renewed day by day.v17 For our light affliction, is but a moment, worketh for us far more exceeding and eternal weight of glory; v18 While we look not at the things which are seen, but at the things which are not seen; for the things which are seen are temporal; but the things which not seen are eternal" (2 Corinthians 4:16-18KJV).There is a quality that comes from skilled strength to stand. We can have power to remove a large rock, or strength to speak to it. The Word says, "God is our refuge and strength, a very present help in trouble: (Psalm 46:1KJV).Firstly, God is a place of security as we find ourselves weak to strength needed for certain tasks. The Word says, "The pride of thine heart hath deceived thee, thou dwellest in the clefts of the rocks, whose habitation is high, that saith in his heart, Who shall bring me down to the ground? v4 Though thou exalt thyself as the eagle, and though thou set thy nest among the stars, thence will I bring thee down, saith the Lord" (Obadiah 1:3-4KJV). Secondly, He uncovers his strength as we are stronger to mount up. The Word says, "Come unto me, all ye that labor and heavy laden, and I will give you rest.v29 Take my yoke upon you, and learn of me, for I am meek and lowly in heart: and ye shall find rest for your souls. v30 For my yoke is easy, and burden is light" (Matthew 11:28-30KJV). Thirdly, we need to acknowledge more time needed to mirror embrace to the divine to fulfill our destiny purpose. The Word says, "My people are destroy for the lack of knowledge, because thou hast rejected knowledge, I will also reject thee, that thou shalt be no priest to me; seeing thou hast forgotten the law of thy God, I will also forget thy children" (Hosea 4:6KJV). This strength comes from deep within will activate your Spirit to soar through the Will of God. His evidence reveals the strength to completely restore the heart desires hidden within you. And, the source of strength can keep high to abide. Throughout our lives surety is able to take a responsibility appearing measurement. There are two different types of strength like building physical strength to working out, building spiritual strength comes from inward man. The spiritual strength activates your spirit and connection to the divine within you. It is purposed to help give you the power to live out the call to destiny fulfillment. The Word say, "But they that wait upon the Lord shall renew their strength; they shall mount up with wings as eagles; they shall run, and not be weary; and they shall walk, and not faint" (Isaiah 40:31 KJV). The divine strength of God is a bonding that develops through faith as an individual becomes grateful to stay strong in restoring faith, and nurture prayer life. Speaking spiritual blessings through the Commandments of God will impact any negative situation. We are to take hold fast to the Promises of God. And, the strength of God surfaces from within before the fitted Armor of God is placed upon our nature. The Word says, "Ye are of God, little children, and have overcome them: because greater is he that is in you, than is in the world" (1John 4:4 KJV). Christ indwells in the believer; Satan has his own followers. Our strength lies in the fact God dwell in our nature to bring us victory! Strength that produces through any battle will rule Satan's kingdom down, and will position his followers to turnover to Christ Jesus our Savior Lord. Almighty God is our refugee! He will not mislead your direction. His strength helps us to stand, and aids to any amount additional needed to surface completely. The Word says, "Trust in the Lord with all thine heart; and lean not unto thine own understanding. v6 In all thy ways acknowledge him, and he shall direct thy paths" (Proverbs 3:5-6KJV). That is a divine strength that will lead you to Holy shouting ground that defines greatness of God through our Lord Jesus won Victory!

8

Fruit of the Spirit

Satan's plan is to stop the Church from rising in fullness of Power. His position is to weaken the church down and hinder the move of Power of God through counter attacks of doubt, fear, and unbelief of division. Fruit has meaning significant reasons. (1) It can mean an outcome to a product given to a Christian. (2) A fruit on a tree takes time to grow and mature cultivation. (3) Dependable trust need for attributes to live in accord with the Holy Spirit. Bearing fruit describe through thoughts, words, or deeds. To obtain eternal life a soul must prove it has repented of sin by bearing the fruit of the Holy Spirit. The Word says, "But the fruit of the Spirit is love, joy, peace, long-suffering, gentleness, goodness, faith,* v23 Meekness, temperance, against such there is no law.* v24 And they that are Christ's have crucified the flesh with the affections and lusts.* v25 If we live in the Spirit, let us also walk in the Spirit" (Galatians 5:22-25KJV). In contrast the works of flesh is contrary to walking in the Spirit. Our conversations, every believer crucify the flesh needed to obtain salvation. Our grievous sensitive wounds are downfall to negative behavior to off course our journey of life. Setting broken pieces of heart, and broken bones takes much love applied to wipe tears dry. The Word says, "For the eyes of the Lord run to and fro throughout the whole earth, to show himself strong in the behalf of them whose heart is perfect toward him. Herein thou hast done foolishly: therefore from henceforth thou shall have wars" (2 Chronicles 16:9 KJV). The prescription to ruin is forgiveness through the love of our Savior. Reconciling indifferences can bring "Good Tidings" to the heart to reach out to the lost without hope end. The Word says, "For God so loved the world,that he gave his only begotten Son, that whosoever believeth in him should not perish, but have everlasting life" (John 3:16KJV). Love is an attribute of God and divine being is his presence. Actually, contrast is the two different distinction of His love unconditional to our conditional love. Barriers build walls that cannot be proven to fall. However, the joy of the Lord is our strength to gain development throughout much long-suffering. Sometimes, a Christian struggles to grasp joy, because it defines virtue. Given a biblical view of joy can be found in scripture. "Blessed are the poor in spirit: for theirs is the kingdom of heaven.* v4 Blessed are they that mourn: for they shall be comforted.* v5 Blessed are the meek: for they shall inherit the earth.* v6 Blessed are they that which do hunger and thirst for righteousness: for they shall be filled.* v7 Blessed are the merciful: for they shall obtain mercy.* v8 Blessed are the pure in heart: they shall see God.* v9 Blessed are the peacemakers: for they shall be called children of God.* v10 Blessed are they which are persecuted for righteousness' sake: for theirs is the kingdom of heaven.* v11 Blessed are ye, when men shall revile you, and persecute you, and shall say all manner of evil against you falsely, for my sake.* v12 Rejoice, and be exceeding glad: for great is your reward in heaven: for so persecuted they the prophets which were before you" (Matthew 5:3-12KJV). The peace of God comes from maintaining love surrendered of our Savior to commit his life for his children. The bond of commitment of love brings an enjoyment of loyalty for servanthood. When a Christian surrenders to life of sacrifice, peacefulness quiets their Soul, to listen attentively to the small "Still Voice of God" to follow. The peace of God borders the limits for the Holy Spirit leading to comfort through any storm. The Word says, "Thou wilt keep in perfect peace, whose mind is stayed on thee: because he trusteth in thee" (Isaiah 26:3KJV). This peace goes beyond human comprehensive. This is empathic expression that indicates staying our minds upon the Commandments of God with act of meditation rewards that certain confidence needed to climb to higher level. Our minds have to bestow particular appropriate place to keep peace. And, follow the "Giver of Eternal Life" Christ Jesus our Lord. Additional scripture says, "And the peace of God, which passeth all understanding, shall keep your hearts and minds through Christ Jesus" (Philippians4:7KJV). The peace of God is a tranquility freeing a believer from fear, and worrying vexation. That peace "guards" the soul, mind, will, and emotions to understanding of the destiny problem to moving forward. A Christian has to stand guard duty to surrender as the gates of entry are open to enter beyond one's understanding. You must occupy your mind on the right things according to the Will of the Father. Finally, keep in peace with your fellowman. The Word says, "Endeavoring to keep the unity of the Spirit in the bond of peace. v4There is one body, and one Spirit, even as ye are called in one hope of your calling.* v5 One Lord, one faith, one baptism, v6 One God and Father of all, who is above all, and through all, and in you all" (Ephesians 4:3-6KJV).Oneness of the "Unity of the Spirit" only comes through the peace of God to serve the great commission. The Word says, "Afterwards he appeared unto the eleven as they sat at meat, and upbraided them with their unbelief and hardness of heart, because they believed not them which had seen him after he was risen. v15And he said unto them, Go ye into all the world, and preach the gospel to every creature. v16 He that believeth and is baptized shall be saved, but he that believeth not shall be damned.* v17 And these signs shall follow them that believe; In my name shall they cast out devils; they shall speak with new tongues; v18 They shall take up serpents; and if they drink any deadly thing, it shall not hurt them; they shall lay hands on the sick; and they shall recover. v19 So then after the Lord had spoken unto them, he was received up to the heaven, and sat on the right hand of God. v20And they went forth, and preached every where, the Lord working with them, and confirming the word with signs following" Amen. (Mark 16:14-20 KJV). Jesus commission disciplined peace in the life of his followers. Long-suffering is a remarkable patience of endurance in our afflictions and trails. In fact, the Bible does not reveal any one certain time. Sometimes, silence is necessary to enduring the affliction or test of trail going throughout our life. The Word says, "Now when Job's three friends heard of all his this evil that was come upon him, they came every one from his own place; Eliphaz the Temanite, and Bildad the Shuhite, and Zophar the Naamathite: for they had made an appointment to come to mourn with him and comfort him.*v12And when they lifted up their eyes afar off, and knew him not, they lifted up their voice, and wept; and they rent every one his mantle, and sprinkled dust upon their heads toward heaven. v13So they sat down with him upon the ground seven days and seven nights, and none spake a word unto him: for they saw his grief was very great" (Job 2:11-13 KJV). Job, however, decided not to speak wrong words at that moment. It is revealed in the following chapter that Job broke the silence, but his speech was a word curse. The Word says, "After this opened Job his mouth, and cursed his day. v2And Job spake, and said, v3Let the day perish wherein I was born, and the night in which it was said, There is a man child conceive" (Job 3:1-3KJV).In a few chapters over, Isaiah's application for a Christian's long-suffering is to follow the primary one, of course, being Savior. His mission was misunderstood to his Servants willingness to depend upon him and completely to obey. His long-suffering, especially for sin and victorious living! The long-suffering Servant is to follow the Commandments of God. The Son of God, who alone can atone for sin walked through rejection. His person is refused, and speech was rendered speechless to the demonstration of God's love for mankind. The Word says, "Who hath believed our report? and to whom is the arm of the Lord revealed?* v2For he shall grow up before him as a tender plant, and as a root out of dry ground: he hath no form nor comeliness; and when we shall see him, there is no beauty that we should desire him. v3 He is despised and rejected of men; a man of sorrows, and acquainted with grief: and we hid as it were our faces from him; he was despised, and we esteemed him not.* v4 Surely he hath borne our griefs, and carried our sorrows: yet we did esteem him stricken, smitten of God, and afflicted.v5 But he was wounded for out transgressions, he was bruised for our iniquities: the chastisement of our peace was upon him; and with his stripes we are healed. v6 All we like sheep gone astray; and have turned every one to his own way; and the Lord hath laid on him the iniquity of us all.* v7 He was oppressed, and he was afflicted, yet opened his mouth: he is brought as a lamb to the slaughter, and as a sheep before his shearers is dumb, so he opened not his mouth. v8 He was taken from prison and from judgment: and who shall declare his generation? For he was cut off out of the land of the living: for the transgression of my people was he stricken.* v9 And he made his grave with the wicked, and with the rich in death; because he had done no violence, neither was any deceit in his mouth. v10 Yet it pleased the Lord to bruise him; he hath put him to grief; when thou shalt make his soul an offering for sin, he shall see his seed, he shall prolong his days, and the pleasure of the Lord shall prosper in his hand" (Isaiah 53:1-10KJV). Isaiah emphasizes the totality of sinful humility mankind. A Christian cannot have divine long-suffering without boring the griefs of our Savior. And, the fruit of long-suffering illustrates the desperate condition of mankind, lost without a Savior. The agony in the garden indicates physical long-suffering in the gospels. The betrayal of Jesus entered a garden, the brook Cedron, with disciplines. Judas betrayed him, knew the place resorted. It is shown the early years, a Christian life blameless passion to serve Christ Jesus can be occupied by evil passions from a heart of betrayal from others. The four gospels expression with much long-suffering of mankind with sickness, poverty, and diseases, but as the people were taught of the ministry of Jesus were healed. Each gazed at Jesus with certain lengths of their own personal long-sufferings from divers diseases, blindness, dumbness, torments, lunatic, and those possessed with devils. Throughout the four gospels there are different measures of long-sufferings real experiences. The fruit of long-suffering is someone who endures something unpleasant for a long period of time. After God gives you the shield of salvation,and working of faith, love, joy, peace, long-suffering altogether the fruit of gentleness applied such as a dove begins to operate. The Word says, "But sanctify the Lord God in your hearts: and be ready always to give an answer to every man that asketh you a reason of the hope that is in you with meekness and fear" (1 Peter 3:15KJV). There are sufferings, and reward for a Christian defended by God to open at the appointed time. Therefore, as God's chosen people we are to be clothed with compassion unto gentleness. Are you a gentle example of gentleness? Sin in our lives manifestations are opposite to cooperate with Him through sanctification. However, a gentle person expresses the speaking of our Savior. God does not operate His power in a chaotic or unbridled way. God has an Order, and Organization in Heaven, and the covenant of God gives us our access to apply our Right to the Eternal Life. The fruit of gentleness does not mean weakness. Through confession of our sins, keeps the door to connection needed open. Rather, it involves humility, and thankfulness toward Father God. It takes a strong person to be gentle approaching anger and ungodliness. As the church fully submits their flesh to God, mercy can manifest His gentleness and kindness to mankind. We can speak words to influence, or inform others with our words to benefit blessings. The fruit of gentleness constrains the flow of the anointing of God to channel continually. Our lives are not to reflect sin, but the gentle attitude of the Savior. Many barriers are from misinterpretations keeping possibly knowing Him. He holds the future, and confidence needed to develop. And, we will stand ready to forgive with easiness of heart of pureness. Jesus appointed the foundation of the church. The Word says, "Let not your heart be troubled: ye believe in God, believe also in Me.v2 In my Father's house are many mansions, if it were not so, I would told you.* I go to prepare a place for you. v3 And if I go and prepare a place for you, I will come again, and receive you unto myself; that where I am, there ye may be also. v4 And whither I go ye know, and the way ye know" (John 14:1-4 KJV). Heaven is reward, a place and the eternal hope is saved. Jesus draws all that accepts through precious gentleness to the freedom of Life. The comfort of "Time Departure" reveals to the redeemed a gentleness fellowship forevermore. The lasting gentleness contrasts to the unkindness upon the earth, because the gods of this world and their molded images are not eternal existence. John the Baptist was an example fiery preacher of the gentleness of God, yet he said, "He must increase, but I must decrease" (John 3:30KJV). God is more concern about out spiritual growth than judging others. He desires our way to prepare for return of the Lord to join him. There are three ways for preparation.1) Confession our sins. 2) Continually submission to Commandments of God. 3) Have faith in God! The fruit of gentleness develops gentleness through our confession. Surrounding ourselves submission allows our worship to remove barriers of unrighteousness. And our faith level growth can produce a higher level. Sometimes, difficult situations can anger our heart to trap from continually enter in the prepared way of the Lord Jesus. The Word says, "Let your conversation be without covetousness; and be content such things as ye have: for he had said, I WILL NOT LEAVE THEE, NOR FORSAKE

THEE" (Hebrews13:5KJV). As Christ Jesus extend His hands toward us to lead through His attributes an extravagance indulgence of impoverishment ruins are removed. The Word says, " Howbeit when he, the Spirit of truth, is come, he will guide you into all truth, for he shall not speak of himself; but whatsoever he shall hear, that shall he speak; and he will show you things to come" (John 16:13KJV). God's design is to separate ourselves from person to Him merely to show his essence. Through His Trinity equal essence separates our will unto His Will to reveal his divine nature. The fruit of gentleness expresses itself through actions of God the Father, God the Son, and God the Holy Spirit. He is a divine person who is omniscient, omnipresent, and omnipotent. A Christian duty is to express gentleness that imputes righteousness. A person who is impoverished can produce the quality strength of richness through the fruit of gentleness and kindness. A person who lives on the streets, which means poor is not depraved. The four gospels expels much immoral or morally conduct through demonstration of power of Spirit. Many were instantly healed through the gift of gentleness. Many examples: "Then were there brought unto him little children,that he should put his hands on them, and pray: and the disciples rebuked them.* v14 But Jesus said, Suffer little children, and forbid them not, to come unto me: for of such is the kingdom of heaven. v15 And he laid his hands on them, and departed hence" (Matthew 19:13-15KJV). The little children responded to the presence of God was considered as safe. Jesus never condemned anyone who lacked the ability to respond to him. Seem though the church has lost the understanding of the loving gentleness surrounded from God's love to touch our painful hurt of disappointments, but it does seem as though it is a breathing wreath round to encircle. Our lack of sensitivity to Light causes discomfort in our souls. The window of our souls squint to Christ Jesus to open our understanding for truth of message sent. The Word says, "In the year that king Uzziah died I saw also the Lord sitting upon a throne, high and lifted up, and his train filled the temple.* v2 Above it stood the seraphim: each one had six wings; with twain he covered his face, and with twain he covered his feet, and with twain he covered his feet, and with twain he did fly. v3 And one cried unto another, and said, Holy, holy, holy, is the Lord of hosts: the whole earth is full of his glory" (Isaiah 6:1-3KJV). Fruit of gentleness was shown from the true Sovereign God to affairs of men. The throne refers to are six-winged creatures to continually to fly in the presence of God. At this critical hour, the prophet attention was turned to God. The gentleness of God was reversing the decadence that begun during Uzziah's years of isolation. His consecration revealed the gentleness of Third Person of the Trinity. As the six wings creatures waved the glory of God backwards and forwards, it swept the mercy of God upon the floor from layer to heights of glory filled the temple. The presence of God surrounded such veiled presence viewing the throne. There is such demanding environment for so that, earth existence hides the gentleness of God. The fruit of gentleness is freedom separation from all harshness, and ungodly speech. It is the ground surface to lift up into the glory to delicate ourselves such gentleness leading to invites others unto the Savior. It has a warm deep comfort, and truth based to it. It is coursed from without conflict of negative energy. It unshackles the shackles of bitterness, hatred, and division that kept out the unity of body to become complete. It produces through the growth process of sanctification of old behavior to maturity in Christ. Additional fruits produce from gentleness in the home environment of families, church, and business world. Fruit of gentleness produces power of authority through any crisis to grow in amazing success. Resurfacing issues to problems through the spirit of gentleness will counter attack any form of the enemy entrance into your home environment or workplace. Once again, remember, fertile ground must plant good seed into the soil to produce. Keep it watered with the Word of God. Keep it prayed over with WATCH! And, grow as the winds blow! Allow the Light work others ways gathering to produce the Souls that are to await you. Serve them with gentleness and a great SMILE! Allow the Authority of God to reign through you. It is vital to your soul. Oh Glory! Hallelujah! Give God all the praise! As a child of God continues walking with God, he will increase the opportunity for his goodness to expresses uprightness, integrity, and morality conduct character. When God places the "Rock" upon you the ground will begin to shake! Run to God through faith, and let him produce more. Do not fear! The Word says, "God is our refugee and strength, a very present help in trouble. v2 Therefore will not we fear, though the earth be removed, and though the mountains be carried into the midst of the sea. v Though the waters thereof roar and be troubled, though the mountains shake with the swelling thereof. v4 There is a river, the streams whereof shall make glad the city of God, the holy place of the tabernacles of the Most High. v5 God is in the midst of her; she shall not be moved: God shall help her, and that right early. The heathen raged, the kingdoms were moved: he uttered his voice, the earth melted. v7 The Lord of hosts is with us; the God of Jacob is our refuge" Selah. (Psalm 46:1-7 KJV). This psalm expresses First, God delivers his people from insecurity to security. Second, God protects a city, and gives his people an assurance and comfort. Third, God call all to submit to his unshakable authority to give confidence. The city of God creates an atmosphere of faith to soar above all evil for his presence to be exalted. The glory reveals his goodness throughout judgements that we are hidden in Christ Jesus. Jesus Christ was appointed Head (Ruler) to sit at right hand of the divine Father God to bring deliverance to benefit his church. He is divinely appointed over the entire universe to reveal the truth to benefit mankind. The fruit of goodness expresses the protection as judgment is come. The fruit of goodness promotes itself at the time of salvation. It reveals the knowledge of the righteousness universally available to all who responds. His initiative grace and man's humble obedience to follow him should shine the glory reigns from the Throne of God throughout the heavens upon the earth. The Word says, "Brethren, my heart's desire and prayer unto God for Israel is, that they might be saved. v2 For I bear them record that they have a zeal of God, but not according to knowledge. v3 For they being ignorant of God's righteousness, and going about to establish their own righteousness, have not submitted themselves unto the righteousness of God" (Romans 10:1-3KJV). The contrast that allows confusion to block the glory of God coming through his "goodness judgements" is the pre-existence for the value of his richness to increase. Many are afflicted unpurged with impure elements of the flesh. And, God desires his people to rid the rudiments of this world. The Word say, "Beware lest any man spoil you through philosophy and vain deceit, after the traditions of men, after the rudiments of the world, and not after Christ.v9 For in him dwelleth all fullness of the Godhead bodily.* v10 And ye are complete in him, which is the head of all principality and power.*v11 In whom also ye are circumcised with the circumcision made without hands, in putting off the body of the sins, of the flesh by the circumcision of Christ" (Colossians 2:8-11KJV). A body possessed by God can be atoned for sin habits, guilt, and values can rise to New Life. The cleansing purging freed or cleared from wrongdoing accusation in our lives furthers the gift of goodness of God. The Bible reveals David's need of prayer for divine purging. His goodness expressed through repentance we are broken-hearted to accept forgiveness from our sins. The Word says, "Have mercy upon me, O God, according thy loving-kindness: according unto the multitude of thy tender mercies blot out my transgressions.v2 Wash me thoroughly from my iniquity, and cleanse me from my sin.v3 For I acknowledge my transgressions: and my sins is ever before me.v4Against thee, thee only, have I sinned, and done this evil in thy sight: that thou mightiest be justified when thou speaketh, and be clear when thou judgest.v5 Behold, I was shapen in iniquity; and in sin did my mother conceive me.v6 Behold, thou desireth truth in the inward parts: and in the hidden part thou shall make me knowwisdom.v7Purge me with hyssop, and I shall be clean: wash me, and I shall be whiter than snow.v8 Make me hear joy and gladness; that the bones which thou hast broken may rejoice.v9 Hide thy face from my sins, and blot out all my iniquities.v10Create in me a clean heart, O God: and renew a right spirit within me.v11Cast me not away from thy presence; and take not thy Holy Spirit from me.v12 Restore unto me the joy of thy salvation; and upon me with thy free spirit" (Psalm 51:1-12KJV). Our sin nature blinds our thoughts, and understanding. The force negatively produces us to think the opposite from the fruit of the Spirit. There are judgements of God that appear unto the new Man that refuses chastening of the Lord as he is developed to walk in the Spirit of God. The Word says, "Deliver me from bloodguiltiness, O God, of my salvation: and my tongue shall sing aloud of thy righteousness" (Psalm 51:14KJV). Until Christ returns we need to live in the strength that continues to flow within us from the goodness of God. Jesus is our Advocate! Lord The Word says, "And ye have forgotten the exhortation which speaketh unto you as unto children, My SON, DESPISE NOT THOU THE CHASTENING OF THE LORD,NOR FAINT WHEN THOU ART REBUKED OF HIM,v6FOR WHOM THE LORD LOVETH HE CHASTEN, AND SCOURGETH

EVERY SON WHOM HE RECEIVETH.*v7 If ye endure chastening, God dealeth with you as with sons; for what son is he whom the father chasteneth not?v8 But ye be without chastisement, whereof all are partakers, then are ye legitimate, and not sons.v9 Furthermore we have had fathers of our flesh which corrected us, and we gave them reverence: shall we not much rather be in subjection unto the Father of spirits, and live?v10 For they verily for a few days chastened us after their own pleasure: but he for our profit, that we might be partakers of his holiness.v11 Now no chastening for the present seemeth to be joyous, but grievous: the peaceable fruit of righteousness unto them which are exercised thereby" (Hebrews 12:5-11KJV). So, however, as we submit unto God excessive exhortation after chastening endures allowance to unlimited goodness to be aware of our corporal punishment simply given of heavenly Father. It is all good! Learning to grow through gifts of the Spirit keeps ourselves purged, pruned, and sanctified for the Master's use. In fact, the new covenant we can be made perfect unto wholeness. In the old covenant, even champions of faith could not be made perfect to wholeness. There are many advantages in the New Testament to stay the course through the goodness of God. We must stay the course, and lay aside every sin that easily besets us to endure finished goal that God has predestined for us. The quality of the faith needs to believe the truth. The sword of the Spirit is truth of matter that will not return void. The Word says, "So that my word be that goeth forth out of my mouth: it shall not return unto me void, but it shall accomplish that which I please, and it shall prosper in the thing whereto I sent it" (Isaiah 55:11KJV). God's sovereignty reveals our thoughts and ways certainly not always his righteousness. The fruit of goodness brings no condemnation, but expectation comes from a life of repentance. It is harm to get across from out each time chastening to better from God, but always know He loves you. It is gracious! He is worthy to be praised. First, faith is a spiritual realm connecting to source of the power of God. Second, faith produces the substance to the needed power for it to become the evidence. Third, the difference between the evidence and the assurance is the evidence of knowing truth. The Word says, "For by faith we understand that the worlds were framed by the word of God, so that things which are seen were not made of things which do appear. v4 By faith Abel offered unto God a more excellent sacrifice than Cain, by which he obtained witness that he was righteous, God testifying of his gifts: and by it he being dead yet speaketh.*v 5 By faith Enoch was translated that he should not see death; AND WAS NOT FOUND, BECAUSE GOD HAD TRANSLATED HIM; for before his translation he had this testimony, that he pleased God.v6 But without faith it is impossible to please him; for he that cometh to God must believe that he is, and that he is a rewarder of them that diligently seek him.v7 By faith Noah being warned of God of things not seen as yet, moved with fear, prepared the ark to the saving of his house; by the which he condemned the world, and became heir of the righteousness which is by faith.v8 By faith Abraham, when he was called to go out into a place which he should after receive for an inheritance, obeyed: and he went out, not knowing whither he went.v9 By faith he sojourned in the land of promise, as in a strange country, dwelling in tabernacles with Isaac and Jacob, the heirs with him of the same promise:v10 For he looked for a city which hath foundations, whose builder and maker is God" (Hebrews 11:3-10KJV).There are additional scripture in text from the Old Testament Beginning to the End of Old Testament on faith speaking on rewards from heaven. Throughout the four gospels many were healed and delivered by faith. Faith is action moving into evidence unseen realm to benefit others. The Word says, "Even so faith, if it hath not works, is dead, being alone"

(James 2:17KJV). It seems though we have a system of ruler measurement without weight of glory in it. And, matters the most that we are not pleasing God based upon truth. The faith that does not produce is dead showing any production can become dangerous. Adhere to faith needs to be the source of power that breaks open to further the belief through the work of our hands to trust God deeper levels to work on our behalf. Faith will exit you out of difficulties to develop an assurance to trust God. And, needed direction will bring alignment to an individual's destiny. Afterwards, through repentance needed to obtain salvation. We need to fully be water immersed into the body of Jesus Christ through faith in the name of the Father, and of the Son, and of the Holy Ghost. It takes yielding your fleshly desires to embrace him, and his desires of grace to love him. Through loving him the old nature begins to fade away. It is a progression that takes time to adventure journey daily living to His creation of existence being to change. The Word says, "If ye then be risen with Christ, seek those things are above, where Christ sitteth on the right hand of God.*v2 Set your affection on things above, not on the things on the earth.*v3 For ye are dead, and your life is hid with Christ Jesus" (Colossians 3:1-2KJV).So, the believer is free from sin, as they turn to a new life in Christ, leaving old ways behind to press on through faith experience of the resurrection power, victory, and over all sin responsibilities. As the knowledge of God renews our lives after the image of God our old habits, old ways, and opinions change to right direction to fulfill our purpose to become "witnessing of power" for our Savior upon the earth. Our life deposited into Christ Jesus, purchased by his blood of redemption benefits our lives to a heavenly realm to follow. It is not wrong to have houses, career, or ambitions. It is wrong to dwell on such means to distract your focus off from God to self-serving, self-seeking, and self-centered pattern. God faith builds intimate relationship with Him. If we do not seek heavenly realm above those material things it can prioritize matters interest to success. Be cautious using not to use unbalance faith for advancement, because it can be return failure. The Word says, " And Jesus said unto them, Because of your unbelief : for verily I say unto you, If ye have faith as a grain of mustard seed, ye shall say unto this mountain, Remove hence to yonder place; and it shall remove; and nothing shall be impossible to you" (Matthew 17:20KJV). A grain of mustard seed can produce from material things seeming impossible situations. An impossible obstacle or difficulty stands in our way to hinder our abilities to full activation of faith. Our faith in Christ Jesus alone depends sorely upon His empowerment. The Word says, "But ye shall receive power, after the Holy Ghost is come upon you: and ye shall be witnesses unto me both in Jerusalem, and in all Judea, and in Samaria, and unto the uttermost part of the earth" (Acts 1:8KJV). The act of faith is fuel to the high commission to witness upon the earth for soul winning. The Word says, "The fruit of the righteous is a tree of life; and he that winneth souls is wise" (Proverbs 11:30KJV). A good life produces good fruit-bearing tree. And, the image of God will produce fruitfulness eternal forevermore. The Word says, "For ye are dead, and your life is hid with Christ in God" (Colossains3:3KJV). Every believer's life belongs in the spiritual heavenly realm alignment with God. Our sinful nature will exit in, and out to stop our new life stored up in Him. It is a working process daily on the fruitfulness of the Spirit in our lives development through understanding applied to application given from God. Deepening our prayer life to become fervent enhances the growth for seed to sow and grow. Through our personal worship, and praise of adoration, it can remarkable built-on to our divine relationship with heavenly Father. The Word says, "For as many are led by the Spirit of God, they are the Sons of God"

(Romans 8:14KJV). Dedication plays a strong role walking by faith, not by sight. Holding on to burdens weighs us down, letting go lifts you above the doubt. We have to allow His love to lift us up by the Spirit. Faith has to be guarded unto proper direction through our speech. The enemy desires to defeat our success surrounding our atmosphere with much confusion to off sight our focus not to believe. Faith creates the push forward needed to reach the goal set before us by God to have strength to run the race with patience. The fruit of faith extends the existence of God to create the impossible unseen. Faith here is dependability, it does not fail. The faith of the Lord Jesus Christ sustains our necessity for our shared responsibilities. Our faith disarms our armor from the entrapment of the enemy to sway our trust in God. Continue to move forward bound in obedience into blessings of God. The worldly faith has to be renounce from old past life all the way. As a Christian continues to walk by faith according to scripture an inspired motivation additional adds a thrust of POWER to increase for miracles knowing God exist. A lack of proper spiritual alignment in our discernment can hinder our accomplishments. The Word says, "Beware of false prophets, which come to you in sheep's clothing, but inwardly they are ravening wolves.* v16 Ye shall know them by their fruits. Do men gather grapes of thorns, or figs of thistles?* v17 Even so every good tree bringeth forth good fruit: but a corrupt tree bringeth forth evil fruit. v18 A good tree cannot bring forth evil fruit, neither can a corrupt tree bringeth good fruit. v19 Every tree that bringeth not forth good fruit is hewn down, and cast into the fire. v20 Wherefore by their fruits ye shall know them" (Matthew 7:15-20KJV). Faith produces fruit to reach needed strait path to course the appropriately concept to accept the impossible. Since many are led by the wrong way, they are obviously being led by the Spirit of God. The wrong spirit can lead individual wrong people to darken pathway. In order to find the path to bring us to eternal life we must know the Word of God. Daily Scripture reading sharpens sensitivity to walking by the Holy Spirit teaching that develops our obedience to obtain fullness of our salvation. Be caution to guard the true Foundation of Christ Jesus. The Words says, "Whereby, when ye read, ye may understand my knowledge in the mystery of Christ" (Ephesians 3:4KJV). Every blessing from Father God is righteousness, and it brings glory unto Him. As we escape the target of the enemy. God sharpens our sword through the blood of Jesus and the knowledge of the Commandments to follow. Our reward is our payoff of evidence that His faith surely can produce seed sown to increase fruitfulness in our life. You can depend upon Him through faith completely trusted through your heart to prove it develops a NEW Atmosphere! The glory of God encounters from our faith after it has been deepen linked from our heart unto the heart of God. And, the fruit bear witness that our faith is strong enough to grow! Praise God for his faithfulness to continue our growth through our journey upon the earth. His faithfulness increases our faith to linking levels one after the other until endurance springs our eternal pathway. Praise God for His increasing faith to believe! Never stop believing. Keep your head above waters, and stay strong to believe His faith is the Seed. It takes much fruit of meekness to keep head above the waters throughout our journey of life. It can define many different ways righteous, humble, teachable, and modesty of honesty to obtain true attributes of a true disciple. The meekness of our Savior is a trail test to be proven, and an attribute of our human behavior. We sale ourselves short walking in the flesh. The whole being of man unbalanced merits waver timely fashioned to interruption. And, as an individual stay connected to the body of the Lord through partaker of communion until His returns, apply the blood of Jesus Christ unto sure meekness to our life. Flesh is not evil, but neglecting to discipline cannot please God. Christians are to glorify in their bodies the fruit of meekness to image God as well in flesh, and the Spirit, both belong to God. The Word says, "For ye are bought with a price; therefore glorify God in your body, and in your spirit, which are God's" (1 Corinthians 6:20KJV). It requires meekness to allow distant change from old nature or sin nature. Death is always signifies a "witness" between the two separation. Meekness is always temperance to self-control from anger, regrets, and dislikes behavioral pattern harmful from others. On the other hand, a meek person is not to go alone with whatever other people want from you. It has purpose to your destiny travel upon the earth to return back to heavenly Father. Our identity serves through our true purpose to obtain Salvation with an excellent performance not beaten down to weariness stead. Gathering up fruitfulness of the Spirit, baskets our deepen need for the love of God to improve us. The fruit of meekness bonds our confidence of heart to the heart of God. And, it has an expression that shatters the negative forces that are evident without strength of power to destroy. It is a loving patience and gentleness throughout all matter of daily difficulties with strength under control developed to define the different from the "world." Meekness is a shift independent environmental change unto God for timely fashion for impartation to apply. In the Bible, Jesus, Paul, and Moses were men of meekness design of God. The Words says, "Take my yoke upon you, and learn of me; for I am meek and lowly of heart: and ye shall find rest for your souls" (Matthew 11:29KJV). That is a great invitation from Jesus to the "world." The fruit of meekness brought Jesus sat upon a donkey, of a colt, and it created atmosphere of meekness unto a great celebration to exalt the Most High King! Meekness caused Jesus to sit upon donkey, of a colt for a triumphal entry into Jerusalem. It brought an excitement of heart to invitation given in village.

The Lord had need of need, and straightway Jesus was sent into the town in "world class." The story tell "And when they drew nigh unto Jerusalem, and were come to Bethphage, unto the mount of Olives, then sent Jesus two disciples, * v2 Saying unto them, Go into the village over against you, and straightway ye shall find a donkey tied, and a colt with her, loose them, and bring them unto me.v3 And if any man say aught unto you, ye shall say, the Lord hath need of them; and straightway he will send them. v4 All this was done, that is might be fulfilled which was spoken by the prophets, saying, v5 TELL YE THE DAUGHTER OF ZION, BEHOLD, THY KING COMETH UNTO THEE, MEEK, AND SITTING UPON A DONKEY, AND A COLT THE FOAL OF AN DONKEY. v6 And the disciples went, and did as Jesus commanded them, v7 And brought the donkey, and the colt, and put on them their clothes, and they sent him thereon. v8 And the very great multitude spread their garments in the way; others cut down branches from the trees, and strewed them in the way. v9 And the multitudes that went before, and that followed, cried, saying, " Hosanna to the son of David,: Blessed IS HE THAT COMETH IN THE NAME OF THE LORD; Hosanna in the highest. v10 And when he was coming into Jerusalem, all the city was moved, saying, Who is this? v11 And the multitude said, This is Jesus the prophet of Nazareth of Galilee" (Matthew 21:1-11KJV). Riding into a triumph, through fruit of meekness spread the gospel throughout their celebration of joy he had arrived. I refuse to look backward from the donkey, of the colt, because a celebration to the New begins ahead! Joyful surrounding of sounds and brightness touched their hearts, the mandate of God did not appoint from mankind. It is established in government of heaven. The "King is Coming" is true declaration of His kingship. Many years ago, I had an opportunity to meet a Gospel Horseback Rider on a journey in a small country town such name

Harpersville, Alabama. The population was about 1600 at the time. I planted an Evangelistic Ministry Teaching from Four Gospels of Jesus Christ to demonstration Power of God with clarity. Each week, I taught and demonstrated the fullness of DELIVERANCE POWER with "Teachings of Jesus Christ." Successfully it grew, and became full in a family country home. Many, biblical studies produced giftedness through the Spirit as I taught scripture text with sharing Visions of appearances. I recall "memories" meeting this certain man riding horse back off the side of Highway 280 in Harpersville, Alabama. He was a white American elderly man carry a large load. His skin tone was rugged, and worn from sunshine to wrinkles on his forehead. Wearing apparel were cowboy hat, blue jeans, and cowboy boots. He had a two sided leather pouch strapped written on both sides "Ten Commandments" hanging over the belly area of the second horse walking along with him. And, the horse appeared thirsty and dry. He was given a certain appointed assignment from God to horseback the "world." to spread the gospel. He was a prophet of God with much revelation, and a high storm was entering into the path he was traveling on. So, I was led to give him personal invitation to our family country home. I opened our home to him to stay a few days for protection, shower and prepare him meals. It was an awesome entry the Saturday morning prophet rode in on our long distance driveway. I was led with a few children to cut down nearby palm branches, and we danced with celebration as the prophet of God rode in on his horse. Hallelujah! Shouts of joy and extreme praise proclaim as the prophet of God made entry. He carried a bag pack with tent supplies and pegs. I said, "Set up tent on any location on the premises, and I will watch over you." He setup camp with his tent outside my bedroom window. And, he prayed entire night long. The glory of God filled my bedroom with great mystery POWER! I could not sleep a wink! He tied both horses to a huge Oak tree out front, and morning brought sunshine rising fun of excitement to see children ride horseback. The family of God invited him inside to share our family such as his own with the love of God. As the prophet of God sat down at head of dinner table, such revelation of Manna fed all that dined. His mind was deeply enhanced with the "Commandments of God" degree. His countenance revealed God speaking to our family. His certain face expression revealed knowledge. His impenetrable eyes changed deep blue as God spoke message blessings one after the other to the entire family. My nephew, stood amazed in the kitchen as we all were inspired through the word of the prophet. The servant did not seem to desire much food, because he had such manna to share with everyone. The Word says, "The Lord bless thee, and keep thee; v25 The Lord make his face shine upon thee, and be gracious unto thee: v26 The Lord lift up his countenance upon thee, and give thee peace. v27 And they shall put my name upon the children of Israel; and I will bless thee" (Number 6:24-27KJV). When the countenance of God is divine the "face of God" appears. I asked, "Why is not a companion riding on your second horse?" He replied, "My wife use to travel with me many years ago, but she hindered me talking too much. So, we agreed she could stay at home and I can call her from time to time." I giggled, "Do you ride with angels of God?" He replied, "I have to really listen, and focused closely riding throughout the mountains, and riding along the side near highways or interstate changes." This certain prophet of God rode horseback all around the "world" shared the gospel for long length of years. He shared "EXCEL of POWER" experiences with my family about opportunities given throughout his Spirit led life journey. We worked mighty miracles few days he camped out at the home. The entire family enjoyed visitation, and few were saved, and much enlighten. Each evening, I visited a nearby University Alabama Birmingham Hospital, Birmingham, Alabama, and increased miracles healed the sick of their infirmities. I prayed for many on the Heart Unit Floor, and a heart patient received a new complete heart. Countless miracles broke out all around the hospital throughout the visitation of the prophet. Each visit I made to the hospital I visited their "Faith Chapel," and prayed for all the families in need of a miracle. And, I returned back home to find the visited guest prophet praying inside his tent peg to the ground with such heavy glory outside my bedroom window. It was an awesome outpouring presence of prayer from his tent. He waited upon my return every night to share the great miracles performed through the Spirit of Healing & Prophesy. The prophet tent glowed every night with glory of God, and the Spirit of prayer ignited my soul with fire of God. Often, I find myself peeking through the blinds of my bedroom window, because the presence of God appeared though electricity had been installed inside the tent. God took excellent care of him as he visited our home. He was not prideful, but full of the love of God. After few days passing, the terrible storm was gone, and saying "farewell" left much joy! The horse back rider had to carry on the appointed journey for God. He took time before departure to call home to his wife, and I spoke with her over the telephone. His wife was extremely happy, and supportive to his calling to travel horseback worldwide. Excited! We altogether rejoiced and prayed together for his safety ahead. I am grateful for the opportunity to bond with sharing our family of God with the sent prophet of God. We altogether were inspired, and learned much from years of his ministry traveling on horseback. And, I prayed for a spiritual healing for her and a child. Throughout my thirty-two years of ministry, God has given me many assignments to setup in certain town to bring the "LIGHT!" The assignments might last three months to six years, and then I am called to new assignment. Paul speaks of spiritual authority from fruit of meekness. The Word says, "Now I Paul myself beseech you by meekness and gentleness of Christ, who in presence am base among you, but being absent am bold toward you:* v2 But I beseech you, that I may not be bold when I am present with that confidence, wherewith I think to be bold against some, which think of us as if we walked according to the flesh" (1 Corinthians 10:1-2KJV). In the presence of meekness, comes great strength of boldness with a confidence hidden determination. Paul had an apostleship and assets authority of God produced through his commitment to Father God. His tone was immediately evidence sign. He had a divine unction from the Holy Ghost to be brave! Accordingly, to manner of behavior attributes of others he was able to stand in the boldness of God. Speechless, Paul was not in conversation with men. He established churches, and set administration of order in the Offices. Paul had no faith barriers to exceed in meekness of strength that challenged his Righteousness. Jesus, Paul, and Moses labored through every hardship, shipwreck, and beating through the fruit of meekness. Moses, title my servant of God, a Staff holder, and faithful man of distinction. The Word says, "And Miriam and Aaron spake against Moses because of the Ethiopian woman whom he had married: for he had married an Ethiopian woman.* v2 And they said, Hath the Lord indeed spoken only by Moses? Hath he not spoken also by us? And the Lord heard it. v3 (Now the man Moses was very meek, above all the men which were upon the face of the earth.)" (Numbers 12:1-3 KJV). Moses complaints against him never brought him out of order to false humility of meekness. God worked along with Moses to bring the children of Israel out of Egypt to the Promise Land. And, Miriam was plague from God with Leprous shame for seven days, and later healed after public punishment. Aaron had weakness of character expressed in actions. Moses saw the Lord's form, in a similitude, which Israel did not see at Mt. Sinai. The Lord spoke "mouth to mouth" to Moses for instructions leading the children of God out of their valley bondage to victor Land of Promise, flowing with Milk and Honey. His good was kind, and he was telling the people what exactly to do. God was there and he was Still, of their Peace. Moses wanted them to "listen up!" Children of God, Israelites delivered through the fruit of meekness of God prepared in Moses. The Word says, "Moreover whom he did foreknown he also did predestinate to be conformed to the image of his Son, that he might by the first-born among many brethren.* v30 Moreover whom he did predestinate, them he also called: and whom he called, them he also justified: and whom he justified, them he also glorified" (Romans 8:29-30KJV). We are told the Bible is fruit of meekness. The Word says, "I therefore, the prisoner of the Lord, beseech you that ye walk worthy of the vocation wherewith ye are called,* v2With all lowliness and meekness, with long-suffering, forbearing one another in love. v3 Endeavoring to keep the unity of the Spirit in the bond of peace" (Ephesians 4:1-3KJV). However, the invitation is open to all to walk worthy of the Lord without living a degraded life to divine call that constitutes the government of God throughout the Eternal realm. Vocation summons our salvation, but we must have patience toward others, bending over backwards to maintain fruit of meekness an example Christ. Every One has a measure of meekness confession after repentance of sinful nature. Because the embraced love of God, everlasting arms keeps reaching out to us. We are never to divide our fellowship with other believer's weak in faith, but rebuild up those with low self-esteem. Fruit of meekness is an inward sign to unbeliever that Christ is alive in us. Our fruitfulness continues grow as God prunes our flesh attributes to grow on His vine. Jesus explains the divine-human relationship by the analogy of a grapevine. The grapevine is such as a main vine, and a believer are compared to branches that are to grow out. There are certain times of season, the vine needs budding for further growth. God is not speaking about our salvation in scripture, but with bearing fruit in (Galatians 5:22-26KJV). We are not provoking one another through boldness of meekness, but need to be subject to one another in fear of the Lord. The Word says, "I am the true vine, and my Father is the husbandman.* v2 Every branch in me that beareth not fruit he taken away; and every branch that beareth fruit, he purgeth it, that it may bring forth more fruit.*v3 Now ye are clean through the word which I have spoken unto you. v4Abide in me; and I in you. As the branch cannot bear fruit of itself, except it abide in the vine in me. v5 I am the vine, ye are the branches: He that abideth in me, and I am in him, the same bringeth forth much fruit: for without me ye can do nothing.v6 If a man abide not in me, he is cast forth as a branch, and is withered; and men gather them, and cast them into the fire, and they burned" (John 15:1-6KJV). So, the Word of God is evidence of proof to produce nine Fruit of the Spirit through God embraced POWER, not our gratification. God's pleasure is not to gain our self-image satisfaction, but his sanctification unto consecration to glorify Him. It takes love to remain fruitfulness to more. Abiding in his love and love one another increases kindness through meekness to temperance self-control. And, fruit of temperance self-control helps us gain entry into the presence of God. By walking in the Spirit, and not fulfilling the works of flesh. As we walk through fruit meekness to scared office, God is declaring our "Decree Destiny" to complete. Further awaken deepens our faith can produce temperance self-control over our flesh. Often, in religious context, spiritual consecration is the act of being dedicated to something. It will establish as we practice fruit of temperance, self-control times needed. The works of darkness veils to blind our minds from being enlighten. An individual has to dedicate their heart, soul, mind, and body to God. Only you can make that decision to live a spiritual temperance, self- control lifestyle. The biblical self-control is the power of Christ desiring God. A Christian temperance, or self-control is not bringing their body passions under our control, but allowing God to bring our lustful youth passions under subjection fully mature to his control. Be aware of what tempts us in the "world." It is easy to stay away from certain passions, but if I pass empty that desire can become a sinful nature option to me. Be careful what tempts you. Fruit of temperance, self-control is the discipline of impulse for greater purpose right thoughts or wrong thinking. We can exercise temperance, "self-control" by saying "no," or for the sake of a bigger "yes." The enemy knows there is something greater in our future. The greater reason to practice temperance, self-control is, because we choose Christ over the "world." The Word says, "Marriage is honorable to all, and the bed is undefiled: but fornicators and adulterers God will judge" (Hebrews 13:4KJV). We should desire more not to walk by works of flesh that weaken our earthly vessels. The Word says, "For what profit a man, if he shall gain the whole world, and lose his own soul? v37 Or what shall a man give in exchange for his soul" (Mark 8:36-37KJV). Everything in the "world" can seem good taste to desire, but a Christian has to spiritually discern their boundaries. As we keep step in the Spirit with God. He will empower us to overcome our temptations. The Word says, "He that hath no rule over his own spirit is like a city that is broken down, and without walls" (Proverbs 25:28KJV). The understanding knowledge of God scriptural reveals an uncontrolled life is not worth living. An individual needs limits with boundaries, to keep guarded within their given God assignment. Fruit of temperance in moderation sense can be showed through thought of behavior or actions. It is a practice of self-control to show restraint to One's own passions or desires. Whether it is lying, alcohol, greed, or hatred functional god needs temperance. It is hard to live pleasing to the Lord without temperance, because we have to seek Him first to surrender our weaknesses to walk in peace. Our flesh does not want to surrender daily. Many individuals think dabbling sins alone we can overcome it will be approved, but it is lack of knowledge of not knowing the whole Truth sets you free. Living a self-control temperance life does not mean I can sin little bits to please my passion, and admit it later to God Cautiously, we must daily surrender our passions and desires through our devotion to God. And, daily meditation, and worship will keep our minds open to hear the voice of God. The Word says, "To the weak became I as weak, that I might gain the weak; I am made all things to all men, that I might by all means save some" (1 Corinthians9:22KJV). Jesus had to prepare for such event, fruit of temperance was not him in a set boxing gloves. It was bands covering Jesus with knots and nails, and loaded with lead and iron as he was bleeding to brace himself to endure all forms of physical abuse. Jesus was condemned to death, scourged him, and beaten. The Word says, "But I keep under subjection: lest that by any means, when I have preached to others, I myself to others, I myself should be a castaway" (1Corinthians 9:27KJV). In the four gospels the Word says, "And they were in the way going up to Jerusalem; and Jesus went before them: and they were amazed; and as they followed, they were afraid. And he took again the twelve, and began to tell them what things should happen unto him.* v33Saying, Behold, we go up to Jerusalem; and the Son of man shall be delivered unto the chief priests, and unto the scribes; and they shall condemn him to death, and shall deliver him to the Gentiles:* v34 And they shall mock him, and shall scourge him, and shall spit upon him, and shall kill him, and the third day he shall rise again" (Mark 10:32-34KJV). Paul was not afraid of losing his salvation, because he disciplined himself to avert any thing that could disqualify ministry, or forfeiting the rewards for his service unto the Lord Jesus Christ. Often, I thank God for great privilege to serve in His mission, and divine guidance given to me through the leading direction Holy Spirit for protection. It is not ordinary designed nourishment manna from heaven. It should be viewed as an ultimately provision from the Rock of Ages. The affirmation expression is intended to supply more than enough! The Word says, "Stand fast therefore in the liberty wherewith Christ hath made us free, and be not entangled again with the yoke of bondage" (Galatians 5:1KJV). "For the freedom of Christ freed us." To retain this spiritual freedom we must stay free from sin. Our old self can be crucified under the subjection of God, because we will become no longer slave to sin. The Word say, " Knowing this, that our old man is crucified with him, that the body of sin might be destroy, that henceforth we should not serve sin" (Romans 6:6KJV). The opposite from fruit of temperance is self-indulgence. When we experience laziness in any area of our life, it allows our guard down for the enemy to tempt us in our weaknesses. We must bring ourselves under constant control physically, mentally, and spiritually to stay prepared for the mission of Christ. A Christian cannot produce fruitfulness outside the structure of God, because it has to come through the Word of God. The Fruit of the Spirit is already in our heart, but we must bring it to surface to manifest. We must exercise self-control temperance until we get to that level of power to stay indulged. Life is full of room of empty space. Fill your space with much fruit that will produce seed to growth! Choose to serve God with gladness as you learn to be broken branches to the root of Jesse. Determine to grow strong branches each fruit of seed that you can "witness" to see! Be a tall tree from the ground up to the sky, and waits for the Return of our Lord to please! Change your atmosphere with much always with nine Fruit of the Spirit love, joy, peace, long-suffering, gentleness, goodness, faith, meekness, temperance. Let Jesus in to change the world! Let your Light shine to glowing before all men. Excited they will become as you allow others to share your giftedness! Be blessed of Him!

9

The Honored Gift Transformation

Transformation means "change or renewal" from a life that no longer conforms to way of the world. The Words say, "I Beseech you therefore, brethren, by the mercies of God, that ye present your bodies a living sacrifice, holy, acceptable unto God, which is your reasonable service. v2

And be not conformed to this world: but be ye transformed by the renewing of your mind, that ye may prove what is that good, and acceptable, will of God" (Romans 12:1-2KJV). It is an inwardly transformation renewing our mind, and an outwardly manifestation to outward actions.

The purpose of God is guidance, or proper direction leading in the "Foot Steps of Jesus." The Bible presents the transformed life is " bearing fruit of the Spirit." A surrender life or submission life to Christ will transform you to become a "living sacrifice." In our daily life we need to learn to depend upon the Lord Jesus Christ, and allow Him to evaluate every decision based upon the word of God and His principles. The Word says, "For the word of God is quick, and powerful, and sharper than any twoedged sword, piercing even to the dividing asunder of soul and spirit, and of the joints and marrow, and is a discerner of thoughts and intents of the heart" (Hebrews 4:12KJV). It reaches inner parts of man's perception secret thought, and intents is such a way behind both to resurface them correctly. God view our life as appeared, not able to hide sin. Temptation can become reality from sin and the wrongdoing practices motives to react to destroy our personal relationship with heavenly Father. There is danger to sin without reason truth without forward repentance to help direct our life right path to stick on. Our salvation involves more than activity. There are requirements of the saints "to knowing God."

The Word say, "He hath showed thee, O man, what is good;

and what doth the Lord required of thee, but to do justly, and to love mercy, and to walk humbly with thy God" (Micah 6:8KJV). His intentions are not for saints to stay unlearned in a valley without reaching a mountain top experience full of knowledge to continue growth in righteousness. Every tear the believer sheds reveals our struggles of fears, not enough strength to trust the hands of God to uphold us in our weakness.

The cleansing of the power of God in our life must involve outwards deeds, and our inwardly thoughts. Our hands and hearts must be cleansed from sin. The Word says, "He that hath clean hands, and a pure heart; who hath not lifted up his soul unto vanity, nor sworn deceitfully. v5 He shall receive the blessing from the Lord, and righteousness from the God of our salvation" (Psalm 24:4-5KJV).A man that displeases God has to arrive to a certain place that he is in need of more righteousness to further goal oneself into the image of God. It is a slow process developing into public acknowledgement as an instrument of God to function manner for the Master's use.

Success shown from transformation without pride will bring our elevation up to new level to enhance glory of God deeper walk to shine inwardly to the world in need of our Savior. It will bring our personal change into a more definitely unquestionable location without doubting the sovereignty of God. We need to learn more about ourselves, and run to God instead of straying away into a spiritual darkness. The Word says, "The Lord is my light and my salvation; whom shall I fear? The Lord is the strength of my life; of whom shall I be afraid? v2 When the wicked, even mine enemies and my foes, came upon me to eat up my flesh, they stumble and fell. v3

Though a host should encamp against me, my heart shall not fear; though war should rise against me, in this will I be confident. v4 One thing have I desired of the Lord, that will I seek after; that

I may dwell in the house of the Lord all the days of my life, to behold the beauty of the Lord, and to inquire in his temple. v5 For in the time of trouble he shall hide me in his pavilion: in the secret of his tabernacle shall he hide me; he shall set me upon a rock. v6 And now shall mine head be lifted up above my enemies round about me: therefore will I offer in his tabernacle sacrifices of joy; I will sing, yea, I will sing praises unto the Lord. v7 Hear, O Lord, when I cry with my voice: have mercy also upon me, and answer me. v8 When thou saidst, Seek ye my face; my heart said unto thee, Thy face, Lord will I seek. v9 Hide not thy face far from me; put not thy servant away in anger; thou hast been my help; leave me not, neither forsake me, O God of my salvation" (Psalm 27:1-9KJV). It takes strength, walking by faith, and complete confidence to soar to high places. Sometimes, it will involve an unshakable prayer life, unshakable tone of thanksgiving, and much patience. This involves in needing to draw closer to

God, and those that need to draw closer to God, needs to resist the devil .The Word says," But now in Christ Jesus ye who sometimes were far off are made nigh by the blood of Christ" (Ephesians 2:13KJV). I have learned in my own relationship with heavenly Father having my own space is extremely important. A certain space to bring me from moral distance, into a new realm of the Spirit dwelling. The Word says, "Thou wilt show me the path of life: in thy presence is fullness of joy; at thy right hand there are pleasures for evermore" (Psalm 16:11KJV). When Christians are traveling that journey path "Return of the Lord." It is important we allow the mission light to shine through our temple to the world. The attitude of a righteous man describes life or death. And, the attitude of grace will express thanksgiving for any changes made from God. When an individual is traveling down the wrong road without transformation, nothing seems to be completed. It seems to be a distant separation from others leading to a disturbance. God is the condition salt to meet the world's need in any situation. He is the mission light to shine forward into the darkness of man's human depravity. Our evidence comes through faith believing our lives are genuine born again. The Word says, "Ye are the salt of the earth: but if the salt has lost his savor, wherewith shall it be salted? It is thenceforth good for nothing, and to be trodden under foot of men.*v14 Ye are the light of the world. A city that is set on a hill cannot be hid.* v15 Neither do men light a candle, and put it under a bushel, but on a candlestick, and it giveth light unto all that are in the house. v16 Let your light so shine before men, that they may see your good works, and glorify your Father which is in heaven" (Mathew 5:13-16KJV). As a Christian endures through transformation it adds salt to spiritual blindness to remove scales from our eyes to be enlighten deeper in our soul, mind and Spirit. It is empowerment charge to perform greater mission work for God. It helps meet our needs, but also gives us a flavoring to help others to reach their goal. The salt melts the coldness of our hearts, the condition and wounds that we allow ourselves to take on from the world point of view.

The Word says, "But we all with open face beholding as in a glass the glory of the Lord, are changed into the same image from glory to glory, even as by the Spirit of the Lord" (2 Corinthians 3:18KJV). Our mission light is not controlled by any form of work of flesh, but the God, we must be led by the Holy Spirit in all aspects of point of life. The Word says, "But ye are not in the flesh, but in the Spirit, if so be that the Spirit of God dwell in you. Now if any man have not the Spirit of Christ, he is none of his" (Romans 8:9KJV). The Holy Spirit continues to dwell in all who are regenerated to stronger commitment to the plan of salvation. The Word says, " For me to live is Christ, and to die is gain" (Philippians 1:21KJV). A transformed life will begin with gospel message to bring salvation unto men. As we spread the gospel message we learn to put off the old man to put on the new man that is corrupt in unrighteousness. Before apostle Peter died he gave specific instructions how to live a transformed life that will never fail.

The Word says, "According as his divine power hath given unto us all things that pertain unto life and godliness, through the knowledge of him that hath called us to glory and virtue.*v4

Whereby are given unto us exceeding great and precious promises: that by these ye might be partakers of the divine nature, having escaped the corruption that is in the world through lust. v5

And beside this, giving all diligence, add to your faith virtue; and to virtue knowledge;* v6 And to knowledge temperance ; and to temperance patience; and to patience godliness; v7 And to godliness brotherly kindness; and to brotherly kindness charity. v8 For if these things be in you, and abound, they make you that ye shall neither be barren nor unfruitful in the knowledge of our Lord Jesus Christ. v9 But he that lacketh these things is blind, and cannot see afar off, and hath forgotten that he was purged from his old sins. v10 Wherefore, the rather, brethren, give diligence to make your calling and election sure: for if ye do these things, ye shall never fall:* v11 For so an entrance shall be ministered unto you abundantly into the everlasting kingdom of our Lord Jesus Christ" (2 Peter 1: 3-11KJV). Our hearts are in need of stretching apart from denial, self- motives, and self-centeredness becomes a painful separation joined through a yielded completeness. Moreover, a transformation life reveals glory to glory of the Lord, Christ in us, and it cannot be controlled by the arm of the flesh. The Word says, "But we all, with open glory, even as by the Spirit of the Lord" (2 Corinthians 3:18KJV). God reflects himself in our lives such manner as he did servant Moses which faded away, but in the New Testament a believer is changed into the same image of God. The transformation takes place as the believer abides in the presence of the Lord. Evidence proven in my own life from reading, studying scriptures, meditation, fasting & prayer development passed forty-seven years. It was a struggle to continue to abide in the word of God, and pull from the god of this world. Satan desires to keep our weakness our main focus, and darken the light within our understanding to defeat. The Word says, "The thief cometh not, but for to steal, and to kill, and to destroy: I am come that they might have life, and that they might have it abundantly" (John10:10KJV). Through observation of the previous scripture, I noticed the words stated twice "that they might have." It is a choice for an individual to decide to have the abundant life. God never forces the plan of salvation upon us. The point option here proven from ourselves is the "abundant life" graven in our hearts to stand the test of time upon receiving it? Jesus used the terminology in (Psalm 23:1-6KJV)." The Lord is my shepherd; I shall not want.v2 He maketh me to lie down in green pastures: he leadeth me beside the still waters. v3 He restoreth my soul: he leadeth me in the paths of righteousness for his name's sake. v4 Yea, though I walk through the valley of the shadow of death, I will fear no evil: for thou art with me; thy rod and thy staff they comfort me.v5 Thou prepares a table before me in the presence of mine enemies: thou anointest my head oil, my cup runneth over. v6 Surely goodness and mercy shall follow me all the days of my life:and I will dwell in the house of the Lord for ever." Walking in the Spirit will develop our mindset more to become such as Christ. The mindset of Christ cannot be controlled from works of the flesh. The mindset of Christ is a mental tranquility of peace that will transform through all obstacle settlement. It has the supreme sovereignty to focus our mind toward the kingdom of God. The Word says, "Then I say then, Walk in the Spirit, and ye shall not fulfill the lust of the flesh. v17For the flesh lusteth against the Spirit, and the Spirit against the flesh: and these are contrary the one to the other so that ye cannot do the things that ye would.*v18 But if ye be led of the Spirit, ye are not under the law,* v19 Now the works of the flesh are manifest, which are these; adultery, fornication, uncleanness, lasciviousness,* v20

Idolatry, witchcraft, hatred variance, emulations, wrath, strife, seditions, heresies,* v21 Envyings, murders, drunkenness, revellings, and such like: of they which I tell you before, as I have also told you in the time past, that they which do such things shall not inherit the kingdom of God" (Galatians 5:16-21KJV). Walking in the Spirit is opposite walking in the flesh. It wars the mind to become divided in wrong action of thought and attitude. In order to transform into the mind of God, needed peace, we need to occupy to right things through reading scripture. In order to attain a goal set in our life. Our direction compass must stay the course of right direction to opening of the inheritance blessings from God. Transformation spend time alone with God enhances the sharpness of the mindset to stay the needed focus for the course until the END. The

Word says, "Finally, brethren, whatsoever things are true, whatsoever things are honest, whatsoever things are just, whatsoever things are pure, whatsoever things are lovely, whatsoever things are of good report, if there be any virtue, and if there be any praise, think on these things" (Philippians 4:8KJV). Look into this certain scripture! Approximately, I counted six times mentioned, "whatsoever." God is trying to get our attention to let the reader know "it is your choice to change your mindset to think like Him." How far, whosoever will come through the transformation to change their mindset advantage to think like Christ? Wow! I feel an excitement for such privilege invitation to think such as my heavenly Father. You begin to think "blessings of the love of God." And, the surrounding atmosphere begins to change gloriously! Afterwards, the refining of the mind measure up to pleasing to standard of God will bring the blessings continually to enjoy. Christians are an extension of the holiness of God for great pleasure. In our daily living, decision making viewpoint needs to change direction to an upward plan of salvation.

A plan that stands upon the "Rock" our salvation without END! The Word says, "Heaven and earth shall pass away, but my words shall not pass away" (Matthew 24:35KJV). Continue to abide in the truth, and maintain a balance Christian life pleasing to God. Learn to gain daily knowledge through the commandments of God. And, engage to enjoy the total freedom of liberty free course in the great kingdom of God. Be diligent in running the course easily beset before you, but get strength through a pure heart of repentance pleasing to the Master's use. Stay measured up throughout your measurement of life upon this earth until " time expiration" to return home to live with the King forevermore. Amen.

10

Purification

The expression from the word of God gives a prophetic utterance of pronouncement with focus on the content message. It is inspired from God to lift a burden from a territory in our personal life of sin. God's grace is much present to enter beyond borders built by men to limit our visualization. Clarity is one element importance to visually seeing revelation of God. God will not allow anybody to change the message of oracle within to crush an impoverished atmosphere in corruption hidden in our life. A Christian willingly from choice has to come into the Covenant of God without limitations. Because the limitation symbols we are still under control of working of the flesh. A believer has to agree to cleanse from rudiments and distractions upon the earth.

God can get us through walls of brokenness, if we are honest. Do not try to live a life that you are not secretly. Lay your life down at the Cross for mercy to bring you to freedom on the other side. He can change our life and make us free from sin. Take full responsibility for your part, and privilege position to seat in Christ. Our responsibility is to keep transformed into the purity of God. Do not allow the devil, or others keep you alter to their sight. The Word says, "For we walk by faith, not by sight" (2 Corinthians 5:7KJV). A faith hero is evidence that "witness" Christ, and Christ establishes the mission call unto salvation. Genuine faith faces all challenges without fear of men. When a believer goes years without purification it allows spiritual pollution to decay our soul. We are an instrument unto God, and he desires our life piece by piece to be pierced from our transgressions. He did bear his Cross with griefs, sorrow, smitten of God and afflicted to develop our lives to pattern pleasing unto him. To avoid obstacles we must allow God to continue set our path on his righteousness. Anytime, a believer stoops to works of the flesh it traps a delay of passing over to the other side. Sometimes, we can get trapped under a "bridge" without proper prayer to straighten it out could be a sign from God that we need to be changed. We can grow weary, and run out of spiritually strength to river blues. Take the time to discover "Life" after born-again. Commit yourself to diligently seeking him for distance needed to make the journey ahead. Apply yourself with instructions given to adapt the next level of surface purged for arrival. The Word says,

"Looking unto Jesus the author and finisher of our faith; who for the joy that was set before him endured the cross, despising the shame, and is set down at the right hand of the throne of God" (Hebrews 12:2KJV). Our eyes are to be directed upon God, and his qualities to run the race. God already blazed the course set before us to run.

Stay faithful to discovering the mysteries of God which are hidden. Endurance persistence is the author's mind to everlasting happiness! The key to a successful life is allowing God to become the Head, and follow directly all commandments of writing of the Book. No matter what level we are on in our life. God can heal wounds, and restore to refreshing to further our position correctly to reach our destiny. After our purification we can gather with other believer's to encourage and inspire them. The Word says, "And every priest standeth daily ministering and offering oftentimes the same sacrifice, which can never take away sins: v12 But this man, after he had offered one sacrifice for sins for ever, sat down at the right hand of God" (Hebrews 10:11-12KJV). The church importance should be a body impact of believers to serve one another, and a stirring up of a nest of a "blessed" atmosphere. When saints continue to abide in Christ for purification refining process it will improve their mental and psychical health to be motivated more into pursuing the righteous life. The Word says, "Unto the pure all things are pure: but unto them that are defiled and unbelieving is nothing pure; but even their mind and conscience is defiled" (Titus 1:15KJV). God's grace provided at salvation universally to all mankind through the atonement of Christ to stretch our faith, and strengthen us to stand in a holy place midst of evil wickedness. God calls his children to live holy lives, free from sinfulness such soccerery, witchcraft, divination and familiar strongholds. Sin will keep a believer out from righteousness, because righteousness saves, heals, and delivers unto freedom from a spiritual darkness. Meanwhile, believer's condition of heart needs to be kept pure and righteous. Measure up biblically to find long length of eternal happiness with God. An example of Noah days, he was commanded by God to build an ark. Noah was considered as a just man, and perfect in his generations, Noah walked with God. He had three sons, Shem, Ham, and Japheth. The earth was filled with corruption before God, and much violence. As God looked upon the earth he saw all flesh was corrupt. God informed Noah of the corruption way upon the earth, but he was instructed by God to build a fashion of an ark. The ark had to be built a certain length, breadth, and height to be accepted. The window and door had to design certain structure to open specific timely fashion. Afterwards, God brought a flood of waters upon the earth to destroy all flesh to die. The window was cut all the way out around the ark under the roofline for light and specific ventilation. God has always had a moral standard of conformity to an ethical style for mankind.

He has always had an answer for a reoccurring problem, but the mindset of man has to be focus with clarity of God to see it. Sometimes, believers lose sight without a vision of knowledge to deal with finding a solution without measuring up their standards to the standard of God to meet requirements. Throughout the story of building a structured ark for God, Noah had to separate himself from the wickedness to follow the Lord. In the Book of Genesis Six, I clearly read wickedness of man can surely destroy soul of man displeasing to God. In the days of Noah, evil wickedness designed or purposed nothing in the heart of man. Man had a capacity to carrying more than a heavy load for their own desires. Our human desires cannot be applied to the direction of God, but is no match to what God is able to change through time spent alone in purification in our desires. Speaking on change of mind from my point of view are many unscriptural mistakes in the body of Christ. And, to follow God we all have to experience a certain place at a certain time to separate from certain things in our life to benefit. The Word says, "If we confess our sins, he is faithful and just to forgive us our sins, and to cleanse us from all unrighteousness" (1 John 1:9KJV). Unrighteousness is another way to say "sin." We need not deny our sins before a holy God. Acknowledging our sin opens the door for forgiveness, and purification cleansing light to purify the heart. When we deny our sins, we are denying ourselves from forgiveness. Jesus is Advocate for all sinners, and Jesus is the sacrifice for all sinners. The power of the blood of Jesus covers our sins with the atonement stain of remembrance. Many people are tempted differently according to their own weakness, but the love of God will cover multitude of sins. God is love! Where the Spirit of the Lord is, there is liberty. The Word says, "If the Son therefore shall make you free, ye shall be free indeed" (John 8:36KJV). For we have freedom in Christ, and not entangle to yoke of slavery to sin. We might not be sinless, but we can become blameless before a just God. The power of the blood of Jesus can set a believer from sin to depend upon the Right to the Father God. The Word says, "STAND fast therefore in the liberty wherewith Christ hath made us free, and be not entangled again with the yoke of bondage" (Galatians 5:1KJV). Freedom in this scripture means "freedom from the yoke of sin."

Purification deeply cleanses us from the yearnings of sin to taste and see the Lord is good. We are not unrestrained from sinning, but must separate ourselves from the spiritual darkness of sin.

At times, the devil will sent spiritual confrontation to the heart of a believer. If the believer is walking full armor of protection you will not accept it. Ignore the desire through purification to yield from the entrapment unto the guidance of the Holy Spirit to be led. Every battlefield has good, and evil. Allow the spiritual discernment level you have to enhance through purification to "clarity of knowing" to try the spirits and know if they are of God. In my own life, I have experience tug-of wars pulling my flesh. It was difficult to turn away from my weakness, but recognizing outcome of walking by flesh created a hunger to turn quickly to God. Because a believer has a weakness does not mean it is a sin. You have to get to the "root" cause of the matter to be cautiously aware to guard yourself until Holy Spirit surface it to mount. On an occasion, I learned to serve others with same weakness to strengthen me to confront my own issue. Keeping silence is not the always the answer to greatness of God. We can voluntary led by our flesh, or the Spirit of God. I search long, and near to open a door. All I was chasing was my weakness of fear running away from Jesus. I had to admit Jesus had to take all my pride, dreams, and intents from my heart. All my searching was trying to be perfect, but what I put my faith in was the need to my fully trust complete in for the change. In the book of Revelation reveals purification inwardly has a reward body, soul and Spirit. God invites the "Bride" to the New Jerusalem. The Word says, "And the Spirit and the bride say, Come. And let him that heareth say, Come. And let him that is athrist come. And whosoever will, let him take the water of life freely. v14 Blessed who do all His commandments, that they may have the right to the tree of life and may enter in through the gates into the city" (Revelation

22:17;14KJV). The blessing of abundance is for all those who are obedient to Come. I thank God for sending his onlybegotten Son, for remission of my sins. And, offering eternal life forevermore! It brings a hallelujah expression of rejoicing to worship Him as King of kings, and Lord of lords over all heaven and earth. In my Father's house there is a place for a child of God. I am a child of God and grateful for all His goodness and mercy. Trust and obey His instructions for your destiny purpose! You are a special treasure of grace held in the Master's hand for his use. Be blessed as he designs you into a beautiful piece to become an inspired instrument to the world. Give Him praise from deep within for changes he has made in you. The glory of God will spring forth showers of the divine favor of the Lord upon your life. Celebrate Almighty God for his love extended his hands unto you. Arise! Worship through the layers of love he has placed within your soul. Worship and adorn Him! Amen.

11

Worship

n Christianity, worship is the act of attributing reverent honor and love for God. In the New Testament worship is a type of submission unto Father God, and bowing before him acknowledges him as King. The Word says, "O come, let us worship and bow down: let us kneel before the Lord our maker" (Psalm95:6KJV). Let your fields be full of worship, and adoration become joyful. When you know you are properly located truly you will feel that you belong to God. Worship adoration lifts him up to enhance his reign increase upon the earth. The Word says, "Thou wilt show me the path of life; in thy presence is fullness of joy; at thy right hand there are pleasures for evermore" (Psalm 16:11KJV). Become a sensitive member of the body of Christ. Build up your strength through divine worship. Going to church is a type of worship, and giving offerings are a part of worship-with prayer. In worshipping, God can open an entry for a believer not to question. He can lift our doubt from our heart fully to trusting him. Worship is an expression of extreme love for God. After you dedicate your life to Jesus Christ, purchase a Holy Bible. Take some time to invest looking around for a church to fellowship and worship. Visit the church length of time to view activity and programs offer for single unit, or family to accommodate. Follow the commandment of God for Water Baptism, and partake of Communion. In the Book of John Chapter 3, Born-again of water and the Spirit combined together indicates growth. New Birth has expression to spread the gospel mission is the work of God. And, Water Baptism is an outwardly expression 'from above" committed change. Concerning the Lord's Supper is distinctive symbol acknowledging you are a Christian worship instituted by God of His Son Jesus death, burial, and resurrection life. We are to be spiritual partaking of the elements with thanksgiving of type of worship" until Jesus Christ Return. It is not to be viewed as a ceremonial service, but as a worship from a humble believing heart preparing for servanthood. Water baptism and the communion of the Lord's Supper are symbols of ordinance, and self-examination. The Word says, "For I have received of the Lord that which also I delivered unto you, That the Lord Jesus the same night in which he took bread: v24 And when he had given thanks, he brake it, and said, Take, eat: this is my body, which is broken for you: this do in the remembrance of me.* v25 After the same manner also took the cup, when he had supped, saying, This cup is the new testament in my blood this do ye, as oft ye drink it, in remembrance of me.* v26 For as often as ye eat this bread, and drink this cup, ye do show the Lord's death till he comes. v27 Wherefore whosoever shall eat this bread, and drink this cup of the Lord, unworthily, shall be guilty of the body and the blood of the Lord. v28 But let a man examine himself, and so let eat of that bread, and drink of that cup.v29 For he that eateth and drinketh unworthily, eateth and drinketh damnation to himself, not discerning the Lord's body" (1 Corinthians 11:23-29KJV). In the New Testament the blood of Jesus, emphasizes eternal salvation applied the heart of a believer. It is extremely important for the believer to obtain eternal salvation prior to partaking the Lord's Supper and Water Baptism. When God has forgiven you of your sins, you are free to remember them anymore. Each believer is called to a giftedness to expression adoration unto God. Adoration is a strong admiration devoted love for God. Time spent alone with meditation can enhance our worship. God takes our lives such as it has been built, and exchanges it for His eternal life. We are justified, and transformed through purification to worship Him to be kept in a holy place. As a believer links together with the expression of worship from their hearts, God is adorned and enthroned with our love for Him. How amazing it is to be called a child of God!

Continue to exercise the faith of our Lord Jesus Christ to enter into worship. The Word says, "Make a joyful noise unto the Lord, all ye lands. v2 Serve the Lord with gladness: come before his presence with singing. v3 Know ye that the Lord he is God: it is he that hath made us, and not we ourselves, we are his people, and the sheep of his pasture. v4 Enter his gates with thanksgiving, and his courts with praise: be thankful unto him, and bless his name. v5 For the Lord is good; his mercy is everlasting ; and his truth endureth to all generations" (Psalm 100:1-5KJV). What is especially significant about worship is the concern that God has for you. "Where are you with God? " Are you with God? It does not matter the social level of gathering you are dwelling upon the earth. It matters the most that you are with God. God does not limit our worship through ownership of material things. He honors our worship from a heartfelt intimacy for him. So, our material clothing cannot compare to God clothing us in His righteousness. Through worship God reveals all material things are only persuasion to believe something that is not true. Certainty, pressing beyond persuasion to believing a lie, will return into a blessing from the Lord Jesus Christ, only to know the truth. Everything can be exposed from our heart to know God, and he will never misplace you in worship. Worshipping helps the believer to find their true place in the kingdom of God. The Word says, " And Jabez called on the God of Israel, saying, Oh that thou wouldest bless me, indeed, and enlarge my coast, and that thine hand might be with me, and that thou wouldest keep me from evil, that it may not grieve me! And God granted him which he requested" (2 Chronicles 4:10KJV). God granted Jabez request, because of accomplishments made for him. As we surrender our will to God our life reveals the price he paid cannot be purchased, nor can it be bought. And, worship brings the believer into a healthy balance to understanding His faithfulness and mercy for us. We can see a hope coming upon arising. We can experience joy that we have been long searching. In His presence safe, and secure in His arms more joy will overflow. Hallelujah! You will desire to be with God where you belong. In His presence the Light will open your eyes of understanding to enjoy eternal happiness that has been hiding! Come out of spiritual darkness with singing! Come out with an exalted SHOUT! WOW! All guilt, shame, and chains are broken through progressively moving forward into a deeper worship with the King! The Cross is lifted up, and the life our Lord Jesus Christ ordered firstly in our life.

12

Prayer

Prayer in the life of a believer is essential communication hearing from God. Prayer is a willing act of total submission to gaining total confidence in God. The Word says, "After this manner therefore pray ye, Our Father which art in heaven, Hallowed be thy name.* v10 Thy kingdom come. Thy will be done in earth, as it is in heaven.* v11 Give us this daily bread.* v12 And forgive us our debts, as we forgive our debtors.* v And lead us not into temptation, but deliver us from evil: For thine is the kingdom, and the power, and the glory, for ever" Amen. (Matthew 6:9-13KJV). This is the model prayer every believer should intend to use without vain repetition.

This model prayer was given to the disciples as suitable prayer. We need to become aware of our prayer language to God. Sometimes, a believer can build a barrier with their faith unaware of their inward struggle has discouraged them. We deeply need to change our prayers until adoration and petition has addressed the attention of God. In the model prayer we are advantaged to accept our Father God to reverence him. Worship of adoration will imply our feeling empty meaninglessness is just a void only he can fulfill. Forever, be thankful for his comfort even though we are not who we use to be before the start. Only God can complete his love he started growing in our lives. Without Him, how would you know his heart? As we worship him the power of the kingdom comes upon the earth to dwell near. And, our efforts developed conformity melts away to draw closer to him. Prayer lifts our head to look high above the nature of man. It emphasizes to bring our conformity to the very nature of Father God to help develop our life to become a Model. Prayer points a believer to the purpose of God, after experiencing a long day. The model prayer brings a believer out of shortage wandering for food and clothing general need. And, he fills our lives with such shelter he lifts our need above our need, not to worry that He is in control. This model prayer fits perfectly as we perfectly are fitted to God's perfection. He is an awesome God! He searches us as we struggle to trust him for protection, daily need of supply, and forgiveness with his great love not denied. There are many benefits for a Christians covered in model prayer. Christians need to bring their burdens to the altar of kneeling prayer. And, allow Father God to express his royal love to confirm his faith still exist to returning our life through repentance fulfilled with a spiritual refreshing more love for him. Prayer is plea for God to take us from where we do not belong, and help us to believe what he says to believe. The believer's attention should be focus on the "treasures in heaven." Even when the storm blows the strongest, keep pulling through with the model prayer kept close to heart. Often, I think of Jonah, his prayer for salvation going to the wrong location. Jonah was swallowed up by big fish, and needed to experience a heartfelt prayer to God. The prophet ran from God, but he prayed. The Word says, "Then Jonah prayed unto the Lord his God out of the fish's belly. v2 And said, I cried by reason of mine affliction unto the Lord, and he heard me; out of the belly of hell cried I, and thou heardest my voice. v3 For thou hadst cast me into the deep, in the midst of the seas, and the floods compassed me about: all thy billiows and thy waves passed over me. v4 Then I said, I am cast out of thy sight; yet I will look again toward thy holy temple. v5 The waters compassed me about, even to the soul: the depth closed me round about; the weeds were wrapped about my head. v6 I went down to the bottoms of the mountains; the earth with her bars was about me for ever: yet hast thou brought up my life from corruption,

O Lord my God. v7 When my soul fainted within me I remembered the Lord: and my prayer came in unto thee, into thine holy temple. v8 They that observe lying vanities forsake their own mercy. V9 But I will sacrifice unto thee with the voice of thanksgiving; I will pay that that I have vowed. Salvation is of the Lord" (Jonah 1: 2-9KJV). Jonah had not found his place in model prayer yet with God. He experienced mental stress, mental anguish, and almost a breakdown to find help from God. Jonah differently had "movement" from the beginning of his journey to the end .Jonah was cultivating his own will to doubt the faith of God in spite of his impossible circumstances. The prophet has an impossible situation that needed a spiritual alignment. The intensity from his storm took himself deeper, and deeper with God. Later, God answered Jonah humbled, honest heartfelt prayer for deliverance, but Jonah had to express his heart unto God.

Jonah had to "look again" toward the holy temple. He had to remember the Lord had all possible authority to helping him out in a tempest storm. There is always a way to come out of our fear, and it is by turning to God. We must examine ourselves daily to the commission mission work of Jesus Christ. Our good might not be good enough, even though a believer knows God. Prayer is the connection that it takes to solving a problem without any solution. Prayer is the way into God unlocking mysteries. Although, prayer can be done from any bodily position standing, kneeling, bowing, sitting, or one's face on ground needs to express our love for God. Interacting with God through communication of prayer is our way to submit our unorganized form of petitioning to the alignment of God. We are commanded by God to pray. The Word says, "If my people, which are called by my name, shall humble themselves, and pray, and seek my face, and turn from their wicked ways; then will I hear from heaven, and will forgive their sin, and will heal their land" (2 Chronicles 7:14KJV). Remember the Promise of God regarding prayer is a high expression of love for God. And, in return his gentleness, kindness, and mercy is extended into our lives unto eternal happiness. The Word says, "And this is the confidence that we have in him, that, if we ask any thing according to his will, he heareth us. v15 And if we know that he hear us, whatsoever we ask, we know that we have the petitions that we desired of him" (1John 5:14-15KJV). An assurance in him is that he hears our prayers, and our confidence builds in his command to love for one another. Personal knowledge is given through prayer from

God to lead, guide, and direct us. And, personal knowledge of Jesus Christ will bring increase of the presence of God. The truth given through inspiration of God will press his love image into our hearts to deepen our walk with him. Continued to love and be obedience to fulfilling the commandments of God to living a prosperous life eternal for evermore. The Word say, "And we know that the Son of God is come, and hath given us an understanding, that we may know him that is true, even in his Son Jesus Christ. This is the true God, and eternal life" (1 John 5:20KJV). He causes our love to increase for him through prayer petition. Allow words of admonition to assure your progress to become successful, and his delight! The gift of salvation of God is free to offer to mankind, but prayer of salvation is the invitation to accepting it. The Word says, "So shall my word be that goeth forth out of my mouth: it shall not return unto me void, but it shall accomplish that which I please, and it shall prosper in the thing whereto I sent it. v12 For ye shall go out with joy, and be led forth with peace; the mountains and the hills shall break forth you into singing, and all the trees of the field shall clap their hands. v13 Instead of the thorn shall come up the fir tree, and instead of the brier shall come up the myrtle tree: and it shall be to the Lord for a name, for an everlasting sign that shall not be cut off" (Isaiah 55:11-13KJV). Thirst more for righteousness, and allow God to be your living hope. The Word says, "For we are partakers of Christ, if we hold the beginning of our confidence steadfast unto the end.* v15

While it is said, TODAY IF YE HEAR HIS VOICE, HARDEN NOT YOUR HEARTS, AS IN

THE PROVOCATION" (Hebrews 3:14-15KJV).

Author of Book

I am so proud to work with West Bow Press, a Division of Thomas Nelson & Zondervan. It is a Future furthermore Right Publisher to educate "integrity" to unmatched readers. I highly recommend a combination of trustworthy and professional support to all book investors. My purpose of Writing is to develop a long range volume to motivate, inspire, and guide text to benefit all readers. Desiring all readers to adapt to a field of general understanding to officially elevate oneself to enter own success. It is a journey of success that will build confidence, and help you to figure out the "giftedness of God" in your life. Your own abilities can express space for reality to show abilities of greatness that needs room to function. My goal for public view is to support value to Biblical standard knowledge that can develop solid ground to stand upon. Every reader needs solid ground applicable to personal growth without a level of defeat from a lack of understanding. I am a Writing with Brightness to Excel your high purpose to challenge, and created design leadership to become significant, view of nature, and reveal hidden knowledge to bring hope to a public domain without borders and limitations. Typically, someone who owns their work until it is approved" Time" to be published. You must stay focus to reach a long range goal. You must be willing to make sacrifices to reach the goal. And, finally be determined to cross over the finish-line. Enjoy your reading embraced with an openness that will lead to next level of Success. Learn to rise high in the skies without fear, doubt, and worry. Take the limits off! Keep fighting the good fight of Faith!

Printed in the United States
By Bookmasters